MIRROR
OF THE
HEART

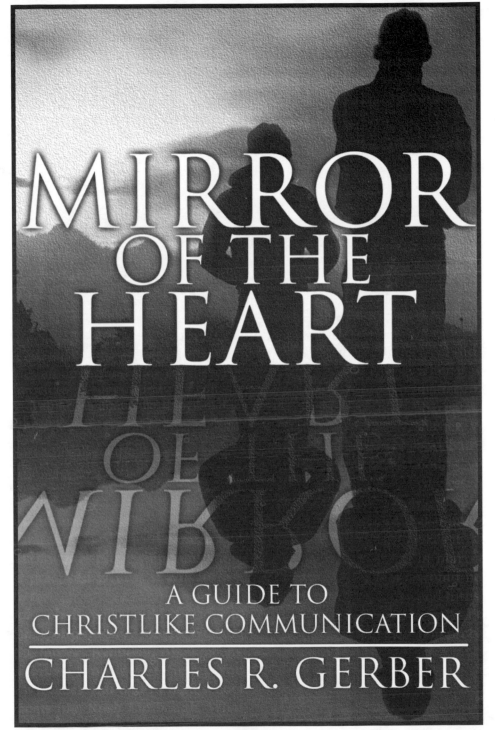

MIRROR OF THE HEART

A GUIDE TO CHRISTLIKE COMMUNICATION

CHARLES R. GERBER

COLLEGE PRESS PUBLISHING COMPANY • JOPLIN, MO

Cover Design: Mark A. Cole

Library of Congress Cataloging-in-Publication Data

Gerber, Charles R. (Charles Richard), 1958–   .
    Mirror of the heart: a guide to Christlike communication /
    Charles R. Gerber.
        p.   cm.
    Includes bibliographical references.
    ISBN 0-89900-898-4 (pbk.)
    1. Communication—Religious aspects—Christianity.
    I. Title.
    BV4597.53.C64 G47 2001
    241'.672—dc21

                                                    2001032523

Contents

Introduction

You have heard it called "chewing the fat," "shooting the breeze," or "talkin' trash." Maybe it is referred to as "bending your ear." What is it? It is conversation or communication. It takes place every day of the year, everywhere from local restaurants to airports, from football fields to classrooms, from business offices to homes in every country. It takes place on radio airways, mailboxes, e-mail, faxes, and phone lines. Communication cannot be avoided.

I recently read an article entitled "Schools Attempt to Keep the Peace."[1]

(AP) Hartford, Conn. Frank Volpicelli had been losing sleep since his high school team was beaten, 69-26 in the state football championship game.

It wasn't the shellacking 2 weeks earlier that bothered Darien's senior co-captain. It was the way trash-talking across the line of scrimmage had crossed the line of sportsmanship.

Predominantly white Darien and nearly all-black Weaver accused each other of using racial slurs.

"A lot of kids made a lot of mistakes," Volpicelli said. "It was not reflective at all of Darien and Weaver."

Administrators and coaches agree. But rather than file complaints with the Connecticut Interscholastic Athletic Conference, they brought both sides together a few days later — over milk and cookies, and finally a handshake.

With cookies or pizza, award programs or sportsmanship summits, schools and athletic leagues everywhere say they are looking for ways to instill a familiar message: "Play nice."

Maybe it should be "*talk* nice."

I heard the other day that the English language is one of the most complicated languages in the world because it is a combination of so many languages. French, Spanish, and Greek are only some of the languages that have influenced the English language. "It has been estimated that as much as 80% of the vocabulary of educated English speech today is derived from Latin — in fact, thousands of classical Latin words came over directly into English, unchanged in form, spelling, or meaning."[2]

Being able to communicate is one of the greatest gifts God has given to man. We are the only animals God created with the ability to do this. (I know people believe Coco the gorilla can communicate, but not with words or emotions, only symbols.) God has indicated three specific reasons for creating us with the ability to communicate: praising God (Jas 3:9-10), edification of others (Eph 4:29), and thanksgiving (Eph 5:4). The gift of communication was created for good (1 Tim 4:4). The problem lies in the principle that anything that can be used for good can also be used for evil. Communication is not immune; it can be used for good or evil (Ps 10:7). Satan wants it to be used for evil and harm.

Our communication can be almost schizophrenic. We can compliment, but also criticize. We can build up, but also tear down. John Powell commented, "It is much easier to tear down others than lift one's self up by achievement. Superiority and inferiority being relative terms, lowering others seems to raise one's own status."[3]

Words can be influential or intimidating (Neh 6:19). Words can be treats or threats. They can impress or irritate.

They can be ignored or heeded (Eccl 9:17). They can be victorious or vile (Isa 9:17). They can be true or twisted. They can be delightful or deceitful. Words can be many or few. The tongue can either bring life or death (Prov 18:21). Words can be reckless (Prov 12:18) or rewarding (Prov 12:14). They can be saintly (Col 3:16), sinful (Ps 17:3), or sharp (Isa 49:2).

Communication affects most areas of life. Consider the words of this advertisement: "In a recent study, Stanford University MBA graduates were surveyed. What factor predicted success? Not grades. Instead, the most successful individuals were those who were comfortable and confident talking with anybody!"[4] This really is not surprising. Jesus could talk with shepherds, saints, or sinners, and relate to them very well. This is one of the reasons he was such a popular figure in his day.

What do we communicate? We communicate ourselves, our thoughts, and our value system. Words represent us like the clothes we wear and the jobs we do. The spoken, as well as written, word communicates attitudes, ideas, feelings, and facts. Every word spoken tells others who we are, what we think, and how we feel.

Job had friends who came to him in an effort to comfort him in his time of grief. However in the process they managed to communicate their attitudes, ideas, and feelings in three very negative ways:

Condemning (Job 32:3)
Judging (Job 33:8-12)
Showing no compassion or pity (Job 19:21)

Communication involves our spirit, soul, and body. It is a reflection process — like looking into a mirror of the heart (Prov 27:19). Jesus said the mouth speaks from the overflow of the heart (Matt 15:18). In Romans 3:14 Paul, through the Holy Spirit, accused, "Their mouths are full of cursing and bitterness." Emotions come from the heart and go out the mouth. I promise that the next thirteen chapters and appendix to follow will be more enjoyable than a trip to the doctor or dentist. Together let's examine our thoughts and hearts to see if we are reflecting the image that God wants us to *speak* and in words that will please him.

Endnotes

1. *The Star Press*, Muncie, IN (December 27, 1999).

2. James I. Packer, Merrill C. Tenney, and William White, Jr., eds., *The Bible Almanac* (Carmel, NY: *Guideposts* [by special arrangement with Thomas Nelson], 1980), p. 347.

3. John Powell, *Why Am I Afraid to Tell You Who I Am?* (Allen, TX: Argus Communications, 1969), p. 138.

4. From an advertisement in *Continental Airline Magazine* (September 1999), p. 61.

More to
Communication
than Talking

Chapter 1

Communication

It's Not as Easy as It Sounds

It's Not as Easy as It Sounds

Communication

Chapter 1

Teaching my boy to ride a bike was a fun process. I would spend hours a week helping him learn to believe in himself and practice his balance on the bike. At first, to help his confidence, training wheels were used. He gradually got to the point where he did not need them anymore. This was a great accomplishment for him.

He was so excited when the training wheels came off. Actually he had no choice but to ride without them because they broke while we were on a ride and still quite far from the house. He made only a couple of mistakes initially. Now, he has progressed to an eighteen-speed mountain bike.

Communication is like learning to ride a bike. It takes practice and believing in yourself to learn to do it well. Communicating is not easy. We may make many mistakes throughout our lives when communicating. At times the task of learning to communicate well may seem impossible. I wish it were an easy three-step approach, but it is more than that. Cecil G. Osborn pointed out,

> The art of communication is much more complex than learning to drive an automobile, or to type, yet we expect young

people in the late teens or early twenties to be able to establish a happy marriage and know how to communicate without the slightest preparation.[1]

Learning to communicate takes place in many places. Much is learned about communication at home. People often model their parents' or siblings' communication style. People also learn to communicate from school and from peers.

Many people are very good at communication. Some are very poor at it. Sadly, some are very good at being very bad with communication. Many have learned to use words as a sharp sword to cut people to the heart.

Words are extremely powerful; they form the foundation of relationships. Howard J. and Charlotte H. Clinebell addressed this subject:

> The ability to communicate in mutually affirming ways is the fundamental skill which is essential to the growth of marital intimacy. Marriage provides an opportunity for multilevel exchanges of meaning. It provides the opportunity for communicating at increasingly deep levels about the things that matter most to husband and wife.[2]

Words influence three areas in all relationships:

⇨ the *direction* of the relationship

⇨ the *depth* of the relationship

⇨ the *duration* of the relationship

It is true that as communication is practiced more, it will improve. Only *correct* practice will improve communication. If it is learned wrong and practiced wrong, it will form a wrong communication pattern.

Can you think of people whom you would consider to be great communicators from world history? Maybe Winston Churchill, Mahatma Gandhi, John F. Kennedy, Abe Lincoln, Ronald Reagan, or Martin Luther King came to mind. You might have thought about a teacher you had in high school or even radio talk show hosts like Rush Limbaugh. What preparation did they have that helped shape them into communicators? Maybe it was just years of practice refining their communication skills. Maybe it was a very natural process for them. The fact is communication begins soon after birth and is learned until death.

Nine Great Communicators in the Bible

☞ **Moses** was powerful in speech and action. He was bold when he predicted Israel's future rebellion against God (Deut 31:24-29; Acts 7:22).

☞ **Joshua** was bold in speech and told the Israelites to fear God and serve him with all faithfulness. He persuaded them to get rid of their idols (Josh 24:14-15). He also convinced the people of Israel that walking around the walled city of Jericho was the way to conquer the city (Josh 6:1-20).

☞ **Daniel** spoke with wisdom and tact (Dan 2:14).

☞ **Jesus** spoke and taught with power and authority. Matthew 7:28-29 states, "When Jesus had finished saying these things, the crowds were amazed at his teaching, because he taught as one who had authority, and not as their teachers of the law."

☞ **Peter** had the boldness to preach the first salvation message at Pentecost (Acts 2:14-41). Even the greatest speakers can have moments when they have a hard time speaking. Look at these verses about Peter: Matthew 17:4,7 and Luke 9:33. Peter was real, and easy to relate to in these passages.

☞ **Gamaliel** had the courage and ability to tell the Sanhedrin to leave the apostles alone. He told the Sanhedrin that if their plans were of human origin they would fail, but if the disciples were doing the will of God, the Sanhedrin would only find themselves fighting God (Acts 5:33-40).

☞ **Stephen** had boldness to speak to the Sanhedrin, and they could not stand up against his words and wisdom (Acts 6:8-10).

☞ **Paul** had the confidence and wisdom to tell people about the unknown God (Acts 17:16-34). Even though I consider Paul one of the greatest speakers in the Bible, he had trouble speaking when he was afraid (Acts 18:9-10). It is nice to know that he was just like many of us.

☞ **Satan** is very crafty at communicating with people. In Genesis 3:1 he asks Eve, "Did God really say you must not eat from any tree in the garden?" This question was to create doubt, dialogue, deception, and desires. In Matthew 4 Satan talks to Jesus and tells him that if Jesus would bow down and worship him (Satan), he would give him (Jesus) the world. It is fascinating to realize that Satan offered Jesus something he all ready had.

A Famous Speech and a Famous Document in U.S. History

Two famous messages in American history contain very few words. Lincoln delivered the *Gettysburg Address* on November 19, 1863; it had only 297 words. The *Declaration of Independence* contained only 300 words. Both of these would take only a matter of minutes to deliver or read.

This is in sharp contrast to many of today's political speeches which may go on for an hour or even longer. This is not counting the political commentary afterwards. Have you ever listened to a long political speech and understood nothing the speaker said? I call this type of speaking verbal garbage. I recently heard that a government document setting the price of cabbage had 26,911 words. Sounds like verbal overkill. To help you understand how many words this would be, this book contains about 33,000 words.

Can a few words be so powerful as to move you to

tears? How about the twenty-nine words Jesus spoke in Matthew 25:21, "Well done, good and faithful servant! You have been faithful with a few things; I will put you in charge of many things. Come and share your master's happiness." These are some of the greatest words Jesus ever uttered! Consider also Jesus' teaching on prayer: "And when you pray, do not keep on babbling like pagans, for they think they will be heard because of their many words. Do not be like them, for your Father knows what you need before you ask him" (Matt 6:7-8). My favorite prayer in the Bible is three words, "Lord, save me!" Peter cried this to Jesus while he was sinking after taking a few steps onto the water (Matt 14:22-32). What a great, sincere, and short prayer.

Conclusion

Jesus taught that it's not the amount of words that matter when it comes to prayer, but the sincerity of the words. Communication is the same way. Sincerity is vitally important when it comes to communication while the amount of words is irrelevant.

Thought for the Week

A great prayer to pray would be to ask God to make us better, bolder, and brighter communicators of the gospel and biblical beliefs. Paul asked for prayers for his speaking; "Pray also for me, that whenever I open my mouth, words may be given me so that I will fearlessly make known the mystery of the gospel, for which I am an ambassador in chains. Pray that I may declare it fearlessly, as I should" (Eph 6:19-20). Paul also asked for the church at Colosse to pray for his ability to communicate (Col 4:3-4). Further Paul wrote that we should imitate him (1 Cor 4:16). We should imitate his prayer and ask people to pray for us as we communicate the gospel to others.

Memory Verse for the Week

"Don't let anyone look down on you because you are young, but set an example for the believers in speech, in life, in love, in faith and in purity" (1 Tim 4:12).

Endnotes

1. Cecil G. Osborne, *The Art of Understanding Your Mate* (Grand Rapids: Zondervan, 1970), p. 63.

2. Floyd and Harriett Thatcher, *Long-term Marriage: A Search for the Ingredients of a Lifetime Partnership* (Waco, TX: Word, 1983), p. 89.

Chapter 2

Parts of Speech

No, This Ain't Grammar

No, This Ain't Grammar

Parts of Speech

Chapter 2

I did not do very well in English and grammar, that is, when I was in junior high and high school, and for that matter in college. I had trouble learning and understanding the parts of speech. Grammar was very difficult for me to master. When my teachers talked about dangling modifiers and bad tenses, I just checked out. I eventually grasped nouns, verbs, adjectives, and adverbs, but after that I was clueless. My grades in English proved this.

I still struggle with it. (The nice thing is my wife, who is also my secretary and editor, is very good at it and actually likes it.) God knew what he was doing when we teamed up in marriage. Without her working on my manuscripts, I would never be an author. She takes my written language and turns it into English.

As English has eight parts of speech, so the communication process has seven "parts of speech."

Seven Parts to the Communication Process

What makes communication so difficult? One possible reason is that there appear to be seven parts or stages in the process of communication.

1. *The actual words spoken (Prov 16:24).* This is the biggest part of communication. A person chooses the words he speaks, and these words should be chosen carefully. As we will see later, words can be gentle or harsh. They can be sensitive or apathetic.

2. *The timing of the words (Prov 15:23).* Untimely words do more harm than help. The words spoken may be right, but the timing is wrong. At times, these words may be spoken rashly. These words can easily damage a relationship.

Proverbs 20:25 says about this, "It is a trap for a man to dedicate something rashly and only later to consider his vows." Solomon writes about timely speakers, "A word aptly spoken is like apples of gold in settings of silver" (Prov 25:11). The consequences of untimely speaking are found in Proverbs 13:3, "He who guards his lips guards his life, but he who speaks rashly will come to ruin." Good advice on untimely speaking is found in Acts 19:36, "Therefore, since these facts are undeniable, you ought to be quiet and not do anything rash."

We are commanded to not be "quick" in some areas. Solomon wrote, "Do not be quickly provoked in your spirit, for anger resides in the lap of fools" (Eccl 7:9). We are commanded to be "quick" in other areas. James wrote, "My dear brothers, take note of this: Everyone should be quick to listen, slow to speak and slow to become angry" (Jas 1:19). This verse is not a prohibition of anger, it is a warning about it. Solomon wrote, "A fool gives full vent to his anger, but a wise man keeps himself under control" (Prov 29:11).

The time of day when the communication takes place is also very significant. Speaking too early in the morning or too late at night can cause problems. I have worked with husbands who wake up their wives to discuss things with them when they get home from working second shift. I have also known people who, before leaving for work early in the morning, wake up their spouse and start fights. Sometimes careful consideration of the time of day is needed when planning communication.

Timing can also include the location of the conversation. I absolutely hate it when people wait to air their dirty laundry in public, and I don't mean at the laundromat. It bothers me when a personal, private criticism becomes a public spectacle. Talk shows are based on this type of situation. This may be one of the reasons they are so popular with today's audiences.

How about those mistimed statements that are "designed" to minister to hurting people. Often, they result in *more* hurt rather than encouragement. Consider these statements and when they are spoken. To a woman who has just had a miscarriage:

"You can always have another child."
"God might have protected him from a horrible death."
"You still have one child, that's more than some."

Painful statements made during times of trials are often spoken in order to minister but fail miserably. The above statements sound like phrases Job's friends would have used. The best thing they did to minister to him was to remain silent for seven days because they saw how much pain he was suffering (Job 2:13). When they finally opened their mouths, they verbally abused him and destroyed their chances to minister to him. Consider these painful statements they made to him.

Job 4:7, "Consider now: Who, being innocent, has ever perished? When were the upright ever destroyed?" Is Eliphaz telling Job that he is not innocent or upright?

21

Job 8:2, "How long will you say such things? Your words are a blustering wind." Was Bildad even listening to what Job was saying?

Job 11:5, "Oh, how I wish that God would speak, that he would open his lips against you . . . ." Did Zophar wish for God to rebuke Job?

Job 15:2-6, "Would a wise man answer with empty notions or fill his belly with the hot east wind? Would he argue with useless words, with speeches that have no value? But you even undermine piety and hinder devotion to God. Your sin prompts your mouth; you adopt the tongue of the crafty. Your own mouth condemns you, not mine; your own lips testify against you." Were Job's words useless and empty notions prompted by sin?

Even his wife spoke against him, "Are you still holding on to your integrity? Curse God and die!" (Job 2:9).

It is very difficult to remain silent when we see people suffering because we want to solve the situation. The motives of the words are to correct an injustice. Words actually cannot do this. When we are around friends who are suffering, we must realize that they will gain more comfort from just our silent presence.

3. *The tone of voice (Job 15:11; 41:3; Prov 9:13; 12:15; 15:1; 16:24; 17:1; 25:15; Eccl 9:17)*. The tone of voice is often an indicator of the mood and temperament of the person speaking. Michel de Montaigne said about tone of voice, "He who establishes his argument by noise and command shows that his reasons are weak."[1]

It is often the tone that is recognized first. Listeners often assume a lot by interpreting the tone of voice. Attitudes and emotions are connected with the tone of voice. Consider this story:

A high-school chemistry teacher, finding the students noisy when he entered the classroom, slapped his open hand down on his desk and ordered sharply: "I demand pandemonium." The class quieted down immediately. "It isn't what you ask for," the teacher commented later, "it's how you ask it."[2]

The family dog understands tone of voice. You can say the most awful things to your dog, but if you say it sweetly, your dog comes wagging his tail, wanting you to pet or play with him. The problem is that people often say the most painful things with painful tones to the ones they love.

Let's look at two verses that deal with tone of voice. According to Proverbs 25:15 patience is persuasive and gentleness is powerful. This goes against our belief that force is necessary to accomplish a task. According to Proverbs 15:1 a gentle word can turn away wrath but a harsh word stirs it up.

4. *Body language.* Body language includes physical posture, gestures, eye contact, and facial expressions of the person speaking. David understood this part of communication, "All who see me mock me; they hurl insults, shaking their heads" (Ps 22:7). Jesus could also relate to this, "Those who passed by hurled insults at him, shaking their heads" (Matt 27:39). Body language can be a very costly part of communication; just ask Mike Ditka, the coach of the New Orleans Saints. He was fined $20,000 for rude and obscene gestures he directed towards the home fans at the Superdome in New Orleans, Louisiana. The fans were upset that their team lost to the Tennessee Titans. In protest they yelled rude statements that prompted Ditka's actions.[3]

A *USA Today* article entitled "Stay Calm While Traveling," examined road rage and the actions that accompany it.

A recent survey of 1,016 drivers identified the number of times they acted out road rage on other drivers in the past six months. The most common responses (you could choose more than one response):

345 said they cursed back
122 said they used hand gestures
54 got into a shouting match[4]

5. *The motives and emotions behind the words.* The motivation of every spoken word should be love (2 Cor 5:14; Eph 4:15). Solomon wrote, "All a man's ways seem innocent to him, but motives are weighed by the LORD" (Prov 16:2). He also wrote, "The purposes of a man's heart are deep waters, but a man of understanding draws them out" (Prov 20:5). Paul had trouble speaking at times because of fear (Acts 18:9). James wrote about prayer and motives, "When you ask, you do not receive, because you ask with wrong motives, that you may spend what you get on your pleasures" (Jas 4:3). Everything we do has a motive or motivation. Every word has motives as well. Some motives behind words may be positive or negative.

Jonah understood the motives and emotions behind his words to God in Jonah 4:3-4. He was outright furious at God for saving the people of Nineveh. Speaking in anger is at times dangerous and at other times it is deadly. Solomon wrote, "An angry man stirs up dissension, and a hot-tempered one commits many sins" (Prov 29:22). Solomon also wrote, "For as churning the milk produces butter, and as twisting the nose produces blood, so stirring up anger produces strife" (Prov 30:33). The results of being quick tempered are, "A patient man has great understanding, but a quick-tempered man displays folly" (Prov 14:29).

Or what about the disciples in Luke 9:54? Look what they asked Jesus on his way back to heaven via Samaria. "When the disciples James and John saw this, they asked, 'Lord, do you want us to call fire down from heaven to destroy them?'" Can you imagine asking Jesus this question and expecting a positive response? They still had some prejudice about the Samaritans. The brothers' question must have bothered Jesus considering how he responded. He rebuked them and moved on to another town.

6. *Nonverbal sounds (groans, rolling of the eyes, sighs, etc.).* Isaiah 35:10 speaks of sighing, "and the ransomed of the LORD will return. They will enter Zion with singing; ever-

lasting joy will crown their heads. Gladness and joy will overtake them, and sorrow and sighing will flee away." Job 3:24 shows how Job expressed his agony, "For sighing comes to me instead of food; my groans pour out like water." Exodus 2:24 reminds us that God hears us when we groan in pain, "God heard their groaning and he remembered his covenant with Abraham, with Isaac and with Jacob." Romans 8:26,27 promises intercession on our behalf "with groans that words cannot express" through his Holy Spirit.

7. *Maturity of the speaker and listener.* Paul gives us a defining trait of mature communication in Romans 12:15: "Rejoice with those who rejoice; mourn with those who mourn." Immature people cannot do this. They have a hard time rejoicing with others because of jealousy (1 Cor 3:1-3). It must be emphasized here that maturity and age are not the same thing! Mature speech will also include aspects like compassion (Col 3:12), sincerity (Rom 12:9), and a nonjudgmental spirit (Matt 7:1).

Five Ingredients for Communication

Not only does communication have many parts, but also Scripture reveals that communication has five ingredients.

1. Truth (Eph 4:15,25; Col. 3:9; Prov 12:17,19)
2. Love (Eph 4:15; Rom 12:9)
3. Grace (John 1:14; Col 4:6)
4. Mercy (Jas 2:12-13; 5:11)
5. Compassion (Jas 5:11; Matt 9:36) — John Bunyan linked compassion and communication, "It is better to have a heart without words than words without a heart."

Communication is deadly without all of these parts! These five ingredients remind us of the fruit of the Holy Spirit (Gal 5:22-23). The Holy Spirit greatly aids the communication process (Matt 10:16-20). It is a biblical truth that the quality of communication depends on the quality and character of the person's heart, which is affected by the Holy Spirit. Jesus did not teach much on communication, but when he did he said a lot. Jesus said,

> Make a tree good and its fruit will be good, or make a tree bad and its fruit will be bad, for a tree is recognized by its fruit. You brood of vipers, how can you who are evil say anything good? For out of the overflow of the heart the mouth speaks. The good man brings good things out of the good stored up in him, and the evil man brings evil things out of the evil stored up in him. But I tell you that men will have to give account on the day of judgment for every careless word they have spoken. For by your words you will be acquitted, and by your words you will be condemned (Matt 12:33-37).

Positive Types of Communication

There are at least four words that describe "positive" types of communication in the Greek New Testament:

epainos: praise, applause, commendation (Rom 2:29; 2 Cor 8:18; Eph 1:6,12,14; Phil 1:11)[5]

eulogeo: to bless, speak well of (Matt 5:44; Luke 6:28; Rom 12:14)[6]

euphemia: words of good import or omen, acclamation, good report, famous, praiseworthy (2 Cor 6:8)[7]

logos: to speak intelligently (Matt 8:8; Luke 7:7; 23:9; 1 Cor 14:9; Heb 12:19)[8]

Barriers to Communication

In the seventy-second annual Scripps Howard National Spelling Bee (1999) the winner was Nupur Lala, a fourteen-year-old from Tampa, Florida. She competed against 248 spellers ages 9 to 15.[9] The word that she won the contest with was "logorrhea." The definition of this word is pathological, excessive, and often incoherent talkativeness.

"Haranguing" is closely associated with "logorrhea." "Harangue" means "a long, blustering, noisy or scolding speech; tirade" (*Webster's New World College Dictionary*, 1999). Have you met people who speak in this form? How quickly do you turn them off? My daughter has said to me: "Speak to the hand because the brain will not understand." The brain tends to turn off logorrhea and haranguing speech within a few words or seconds. These two types of speech will halt all effective communication.

Barriers to effective communication deflect and defeat the real purpose of communication. D. Corydon Hammond, Dean H. Hepworth, and Veon G. Smith list several of them:

passivity
dominance of one of the people in the relationship
inappropriate self-disclosure
interrogation or grilling
distancing patterns for security
    taboos against crying
    skirting uncomfortable issues
    false reassurance
    emotional detachment, disconnection, and indifference
    intellectualization
crude language
jargon that has split definitions
moralizing, judging, and condemning
inept confrontation
    arguing
    dogmatic interpretation
pressure tactics[10]

People utilize these barriers sometimes on a daily basis to prevent communication from fulfilling its purpose.

Besides setting up barriers to communication, we can

altogether destroy it. Dr. Henry Brandt[11] has three "communication killers" that people use for self-protection. They are:

✡ *Explosion*—which is the first defensive weapon against possible harmful communication. When people are expecting harm, this produces fear which can prompt an anger response. People can also use explosion as a way of saying, "Don't go there, or don't go any further."

✡ *Tears*—which can be used as a way of saying, "Don't communicate negatives with me or I will cry." This is not true of all tears! People need to be able to differentiate between tears of joy, pain, stress, hurt, and manipulation.

✡ *Silence*—which stops communication by providing no feedback and nothing which the other person can respond to.

We often raise other common barriers when we wish to prevent open and sincere communication.

☎ patronizing remarks
☎ condescending statements and attitudes
☎ trivializing what the other person is saying
☎ interrupting the flow by asking questions or making statements that are out of context
☎ correcting a person's grammar while he is speaking
☎ shaking your head while someone is speaking to you
☎ finding fault with every statement
☎ communication diversion

Anger, jealousy, and hatred as barriers have a unique effect on communication. In 2 Samuel 13 David's family shut down communication with extreme results. Absalom hated his brother because of what Amnon did to Absalom's sister sexually. Absalom did not talk to his brother, Amnon, for two years. We know from his account that Absalom plotted revenge and eventually killed Amnon. This tragic story highlights the devastating effects of anger and hatred.

Hatred can also prompt evil, wicked communication.

Joseph's brothers hated him and were jealous of him. They could not speak kindly to him (Gen 37:4). These brothers eventually let their hatred escalate to the point where they sold their own brother into slavery. People despised Saul when he became king and said, "How can this fellow save us?" They also brought the new king no gifts. In other words, they refused to show respect and honor to him (1 Sam 10:26-27).

The subject matter being discussed can often be an additional barrier to communication. There are many topics people would feel uncomfortable discussing. Whether a particular subject is uncomfortable would also be dependent upon who the listener is. For example, children might have a difficult time talking to parents about a wide variety of topics. Some of them may be:

> contraceptive use and knowledge
> sexual activity and values
> abortion
> alcohol and drug use
> stealing from a store
> being part of a gang
> guns and knives in school

These topics are stressful to discuss with parents due to at least two emotions:

> *Fear* of possible rejection, ridicule, abandonment, exposure (Acts 18:9);
> *Hatred/anger/resentment* that could be created by strong disagreements which could arise from the discussion.

Conclusion

You don't need to be an expert in grammar to learn to be an expert in communication. Your heartfelt desire to be a heart healer means more than all the perfectly written and syntactically crafted speeches you write or deliver. Trust the Lord Jesus to teach you what to say in your moments of need as a surrendered disciple of speech.

Thought for the Week

The best way to improve your communication is to improve the thoughts of the heart. By far the best way to improve the thoughts of the heart is to put the word of God in it daily. Paul wrote, "Let the word of Christ dwell in you richly . . . ." (Col 3:16). This will greatly enhance communication.

What could you do to improve the thoughts of your heart?

Memory Verses for the Week

"Don't you see that whatever enters the mouth goes into the stomach and then out of the body? But the things that come out of the mouth come from the heart, and these make a man 'unclean'" (Matt 15:17-18).

"Kings take pleasure in honest lips; they value a man who speaks the truth" (Prov 16:13).

Endnotes

1. Les Parrott III, *High-Maintenance Relationships: How to Handle Impossible People* (Wheaton, IL: Tyndale, 1996), p. 56.

2. From the *Des Moines Tribune* quoted in Paul Lee Tan, *Encyclopedia of 7,700 Illustrations: Signs of the Times* (Rockville, MD: Assurance Publishers, 1984), p. 1411.

3. Condensed from *The StarPress*, Muncie, IN (October 19, 1999).

4. *USA Today* (November 24-25, 1999).

5. Spiros Zodhiates, *The Complete Word Study Dictionary — New Testament* (Chattanooga, TN: AMG, 1992), p. 611.

6. Ibid., p. 677.

7. Ibid., p. 686.

8. Ibid., p. 924.

9. Paraphrased from the Associated Press, *The StarPress*, Muncie, IN, (June 4, 1999).

10. Condensed from D. Corydon Hammond, Dean H. Hepworth, and Veon G. Smith, *Improving Therapeutic Communication* (San Francisco: Jossey-Bass Publishers, 1978), pp. 66-79.

11. Condensed from Tim LaHaye, *How to be Happy through Marriage* (Wheaton, IL: Tyndale, 1971), pp. 118-120.

Chapter 3

Gender, Personality, and Communication

Gender, Personality, and Communication

Chapter 3

Let's dare to look at gender, personality, and communication. I recently received an e-mail titled "Advantages to Being a Man." Several of them dealt with communication:

> You can quietly watch a game with your buddy for hours without thinking: "He must be mad at me."
>
> You can quietly enjoy a car ride from the passenger's seat.
>
> Your pals can be trusted never to trap you with, "So, notice anything different about the way I look?"

As funny as the above e-mail may be, it also may be true! Satan is an opportunist, and he will exploit this difference between men and women (Luke 4:13). His goal is to create division and a civil war within the home, resulting in ruin (Matt 12:25). To prove the point about how sexual genders communicate differently, why do moms typically get along better with their sons and dads with their daughters? Conflict, disagreement, and division tend to follow in same sex patterns. Communication conflicts can also follow this pattern. Jealousy and competition in relationships can greatly affect communication in harmful ways.

Communication and Personality Types

A large influence on communication is personality. Carl Jung originally came up with the common personality terms introvert and extrovert. Hans Eysenck later did research on these two personality types. He said about extroverts:

> The typical extrovert is sociable, likes parties, has many friends, needs to have people to talk to, and does not like reading or studying by himself. He craves excitement, takes chances, often sticks his neck out, acts on the spur of the moment, and is generally an impulsive individual. He is fond of practical jokes, always has a ready answer, and generally likes change; is carefree, easygoing, optimistic, and "likes to laugh and be merry." He prefers to keep moving and doing things, tends to be aggressive and lose his temper quickly; altogether his feelings are not kept under tight control, and he is not always a reliable person.[1]

About introverts Eysenck said:

> The typical introvert is a quiet, retiring sort of person, intro-spective, fond of books rather than people; he is reserved and distant except to intimate friends. He tends to plan ahead, "looks before he leaps," and mistrusts the impulse of the moment. He does not like excitement, takes matters of every-day life with proper seriousness and likes a well-ordered mode of life. He keeps his feelings under close control, seldom behaves in an aggressive manner, and does not lose his temper easily. He is reliable, somewhat pessimistic and places great value on ethical standards.[2]

In general, when it comes to communication, extroverts:

1. communicate with energy and enthusiasm
2. respond quickly, without a long time to think
3. usually focus on things or people in communicating
4. like to communicate to groups
5. like face-to-face communication

6. might tend to think out loud before coming to a conclusion in meetings

Introverts will communicate in a different manner. Introverts do the following when communicating:

1. keep energy and enthusiasm inside
2. think before responding
3. focus on internal thoughts and ideas
4. need to be drawn out
5. seek one-to-one communication
6. like written communication
7. think for a long time before speaking thoughts out in meetings[3]

Gary Smalley and Dr. John Trent give four personality types: lion, beaver, otter, and golden retriever.

Lions are "Let's do it now"
Beavers are "How was it done in the past?"
Otters are "Trust me! It'll work out"
Golden retrievers are "Let's keep things the way they are."[4]

In communication,

Lions want *"Reader's Digest*-length communication" and often feel challenged by questions. They are not afraid of pressure or confrontation.[5]
Beavers tend to keep a close watch on their emotions and focus on the past.[6]
Otters tend to avoid the fine points and avoid confrontation.[7]
Golden retrievers have a strong need for close relationships and are compassionate.[8]

All personalities have weaknesses and misperceptions in communication. Not being talkative can be seen as disrespectful, cold, or stuck up. Overtalkativeness could be seen as being domineering or bossy. These can be misleading labels. A hasty judgment based on minimal conversations should not be a permanent conclusion about that person.

God made individual personalities, and they are all good (1 Tim 4:4). People, at times, can internally criticize themselves for their personality type. This only makes communication more stressful. It is important to learn to accept your personality as a gift from God (Rom 15:7).

Gender and Communication

Not only are there personality differences in communication, there are also gender differences. Women typically feel that things are improving when they are talking about an issue. Men tend to think that when issues are not discussed, everything is OK. Statisticians estimate that men speak approximately 25,000 words a day while women speak about 30,000. Women want to talk; men don't feel it is as necessary. This can create friction in a relationship. Women tend to be more intuitive and base decisions on feelings. Men tend to look at the facts and submerge their feelings. Do you think that Satan takes advantage of these differences? How?

If your spouse tells you that he or she thinks you are working too long and that he or she would like to spend some time with you, would this be seen as a complaint or a compliment? Would the answer be different according to gender? If the woman says this to her husband, the man might see it as a complaint. But, if the man would say that to his wife, she would see it as a compliment and would be very happy that her husband wants to spend time with her. This statement could be interpreted or misinterpreted as disrespectful, condescending, cold, unsupportive, and uncaring. Actually it is a compliment! Isn't it strange that what can be seen as a compliment can also be seen as a criticism?

Are tears masculine or feminine? Do men have a hard time dealing with the tears of others? If a man can cry in front of others, is it an indication that he is secure with who he is?

Men typically want to fix things. Women typically ask just that someone listen to what they are saying. Can you see where this would cause some natural friction between the sexes? I am sure that Satan takes full advantage of this.

Gender differences in communication will always exist. Though the varying interpretations can sometimes create frustration, they can also lead to a fuller communication process. Husband and wife can learn to appreciate the multiple viewpoints expressed in a conversation.

The Sharing Process of Communication

Communication is a transparent process of sharing. It makes people open and vulnerable to others — vulnerable to hurt but also vulnerable to love. In order to have open lines of communication, three elements are necessary: safety, ease, and no fear of harm (Prov 1:33). As people feel more safety, ease, and less harm, people can have deepening communication levels. John Powell gives five levels of communication:

1. cliché conversation
2. reporting facts about others
3. my ideas and judgments
4. my feelings and emotions
5. peak communication — absolute openness and honesty with empathy.[9]

As you go deeper in the levels of communication, you become more open to criticism. But, you also open yourself up to deeper, lasting relationships as well. Paul understood this when he wrote, "We loved you so much that we were delighted to share with you not only the gospel of God but our lives as well, because you had become so dear to us" (1 Thess 2:8). He added that he longed to see them and to strengthen their faith (1 Thess 3:10). These are examples of the fourth or fifth level of communication.

Is prayer a form of communication? Obviously we are talking to God, but we often pray for other people and their needs. When we pray for others, we allow God to see our love and concern for others. We are completely open to God's working in our own lives as well. True fellowship with God involves the last two levels of communication.

Many people never get to the fifth level in their communication process. This can be due to fear of rejection or abandonment. It also might be due to past criticism they have faced. Because of past communication failures, many people never allow themselves to open up to experience deeper communion.

Paul mentioned that love and sharing together (1 Thess 2:8) were important to him and his ministry. Sharing is important to every relationship. If we don't share our needs, joys, concerns, or praises with our Christian brothers and sisters, we deny them the opportunity to share in our pilgrimage of faith (Gal 6:2).

Often, intimate sharing is restricted to a small number of people. Jesus was very close to three of the disciples: Peter, James, and John. When he raised Jairus' daughter, only Peter, James, and John were allowed to be present (Mark 5:35-43). At Christ's transfiguration, only these three were with Jesus (Mark 9:2). He shared the sorrow caused by his pending death with this inner circle (Matt 26:37). Why do you think he only shared this pain with three disciples and not all twelve? Did Jesus feel that he could confide in these people? Did Jesus trust these three disciples more than the others? Did these three disciples care more about Jesus than the others? Have you ever considered the number of people you really share with? The number is probably not more than two or three. It is normal for people to have a smaller number of close friends and a larger number of acquaintances.

Thoughts for the Week

God is the creator of personalities. He does not see one personality as being better or healthier than another one.

Make room in your heart for the people to whom you talk. Open wide your heart to them and allow them to get close.

Memory Verse for the Week

"My mouth is filled with your praise, declaring your splendor all day long" (Ps 71:8).

Endnotes

1. Walter Mischel, *Introductions to Personality*, 2nd ed. (New York: Holt, Rinehart and Winston, 1979), p. 21.

2. Ibid., p. 22.

3. Adapted from Jean Kummerow, *Talking in Type* (Center for Applications of Psychological Type, 1985).

4. Condensed from Gary Smalley and John Trent, *The Two Sides of Love* (Pomona, CA: Focus on the Family Publishing, 1990), p. 35.

5. Ibid., pp. 35-37.

6. Ibid., pp. 52, 65.

7. Ibid., pp. 74, 78.

8. Ibid., pp. 87, 89.

9. Powell, *Why Am I Afraid*, pp. 54-62.

Unprofitable
Communication

Chapter 4

Walking with Your Hands behind Your Back

"That's Not What I Said!"

"That's Not What I Said!"

Walking with Your Hands behind Your Back

Chapter 4

Any behavior is subject to interpretation, which means the interpretation could also be wrong. The old adage that there are always two sides to every story is true when interpreting behaviors. Some of David's men experienced this first hand in 2 Samuel 10:1-4. Consider what happened when David's good intentions were misconstrued:

> In the course of time, the king of the Ammonites died, and his son Hanun succeeded him as king. David thought, "I will show kindness to Hanun son of Nahash, just as his father showed kindness to me." So David sent a delegation to express his sympathy to Hanun concerning his father.
> When David's men came to the land of the Ammonites, the Ammonite nobles said to Hanun their lord, "Do you think David is honoring your father by sending men to you to express sympathy? Hasn't David sent them to you to explore the city and spy it out and overthrow it?" So Hanun seized David's men, shaved off half of each man's beard, cut off their garments in the middle at the buttocks, and sent them away.

David's true intention was to minister to the new king who had just lost his father. David had sympathy for Hanun. Hanun misinterpreted what was being done because he listened to his advisers who considered the gesture a possible threat. So Hanun humiliated the men, and they walked back home with their hands behind their backs hiding their bare buttocks.

What effect did this treatment have on the mental and emotional well-being of the envoys? "When David was told about this, he sent messengers to meet the men, for they were greatly humiliated. The king said, 'Stay at Jericho till your beards have grown, and then come back'" (2 Sam 10:5). What was David's reaction? "On hearing this, David sent Joab out with the entire army of fighting men. The Ammonites came out and drew up in battle formation at the entrance to their city gate, while the Arameans of Zobah and Rehob and the men of Tob and Maacah were by themselves in the open country" (2 Sam 10:7-8).

The consequences of Hanun's misinterpretation were horrible. "When David was told of this, he gathered all Israel, crossed the Jordan and went to Helam. The Arameans formed their battle lines to meet David and fought against him. But they fled before Israel, and David killed seven hundred of their charioteers and forty thousand of their foot soldiers. He also struck down Shobach the commander of their army, and he died there" (2 Sam 10:17-18).

Six Assumptions

The reason for miscommunication depends on assumptions and analyses of both the listener and speaker. Between a word being spoken and its being understood by the hearer, there are six opportunities for miscommunication to take place.

1. What I said.
2. What I thought I said.
3. What you thought I said.
4. What you said.

5. What you thought you said.

6. What I thought you said.

Words are symbols representing things, actions, and concepts. The dictionary informs us of the ideas and concepts these symbols stand for. You'll notice that more often than not, a word will have several possible definitions. Sometimes the difference in meaning between definitions is very subtle. This can lead to misunderstanding. These meanings are further colored by our own experiences which influence how we understand a particular word. The shades of meaning can be infinite. The shading I put on the meaning of a word can be quite different from the shade you attribute to it. Within these varieties of definitions and shades of shades of meanings is a vast room allowing for grave misunderstandings. It is this variety which provides the fertile ground for puns and double entendres. That is why it is amazing we understand each other clearly as often as we do!

Famous Communication Bloopers

Getting at the intended meaning of any communication is a challenge. It is this fact alone that probably causes some of the worst communication scenarios. I recently received an e-mail illustrating some well-intentioned sentiments gone awry.

Question: "If you could live forever, would you and why?"
Answer: "I would not live forever, because we should not live forever, because if we were supposed to live forever, then we would live forever, but we cannot live forever, which is why I would not live forever" Miss Alabama in the 1994 Miss USA contest.

"Smoking kills. If you're killed, you've lost a very important part of your life" Brooke Shields, during an interview to become spokesperson for a federal anti-smoking campaign.

"I've never had major knee surgery on any other part of my

body" Winston Bennett, University of Kentucky basketball forward.

"We're going to turn this team around 360 degrees" Jason Kidd, upon his drafting to the Dallas Mavericks.

"Half this game is ninety percent mental" Philadelphia Phillies manager, Danny Ozark.

"It isn't pollution that's harming the environment. It's the impurities in our air and water that are doing it" Former U.S. Vice President Dan Quayle.

"I love California. I practically grew up in Phoenix" Former U.S. Vice President Dan Quayle.

"It's no exaggeration to say that the undecideds could go one way or another" George Bush, former U.S. President.

"I have opinions of my own—strong opinions—but I don't always agree with them" George Bush, former U.S. President.

"The word 'genius' isn't applicable in football. A genius is a guy like Norman Einstein" Joe Theisman, NFL football quarterback and sports analyst.

"Traditionally, most of Australia's imports come from overseas" Keppel Enderbery.

"We apologize for the error in last week's paper in which we stated that Mr. Arnold Dogbody was a defective in the police force. We meant, of course, that Mr. Dogbody is a detective in the police farce" Correction Notice in the *Ely Standard*, a British newspaper.

Let me prove my point about finding the intended meaning. A friend of yours has just said "I really like *Twister.*" How can this be interpreted or misinterpreted? Is he saying he likes the party game with the color-dotted mat? Is he saying he likes the big hit movie about tornadoes? Or is he saying he likes the new type of juice drinks that are a combination of two or three juices in one?

Here is another example. Your friend runs into the room yelling, "The beetles are coming!" Is he referring to an infestation of insects? Or perhaps he's talking about the return of the small car produced by Volkswagen. Or has the local discount store bought a huge shipment of retro albums by the English singing sensations of the '60s and '70s?

Communication of all kinds can be very humorous. Written communication can be exceptionally funny. Consider the following quotes of actual statements from insurance accident forms in which people were asked to use as few words as possible.

The other car collided with mine without giving warnings of its intentions.

Coming home, I drove into the wrong house and collided with a tree I didn't have.

I thought my window was down, but I found out it was up when I put my hand through it.

I collided with a stationary truck coming the other way.

The truck backed into the windshield into my wife's face.

A pedestrian hit me and went under my car.

The guy was all over the road. I had to swerve a number of times before I hit him.

I pulled away from the side road, glanced at my mother-in-law and headed for the embankment.

The pedestrian had no idea which direction to run, so I ran over him.

I saw a slow-moving, sad-faced old gentleman as he bounced off the hood of my car.

The telephone pole was approaching. I was attempting to swerve out of its way, when it struck my front end.

I was on my way to the doctor with rear end trouble when my universal joint gave way causing me to have this accident.

I had been driving for 40 years when I fell asleep at the wheel.

Mixed Signals

The other day I was driving home from my office and I saw some used bikes for sale. One was a girl's bike; it was painted with my daughter's favorite colors — purple and pink. When I drove into the driveway I saw the bike, a for sale sign, a big dog unchained on the porch, a goat tied to a tree, and a "no trespassing" sign on another tree. I did not get out the car. I simply put my car in reverse and took off. I was greatly confused by the mixed signals I received at this house. I did figure out why no one was buying this bike. The "for sale" sign was very attractive, but the "big dog" and the "no trespassing" signs discouraged would-be buyers.

Miscommunication of this type seems to have several possible sources. Poorly chosen words and flawed communication styles are just two contributors to miscommunication. "Doublespeak is one of the biggest problems in the English language," according to a National Council of Teachers state-of-the-language report. "Doublespeak" is the very prevalent tendency in business and politics to write convoluted labels for events and ideas to keep them from sounding so harsh. Politically correct language is one form of this. The report cited the following examples: "One stockbroker called the October 1987 stock market crash a 'fourth quarter equity retreat.' The Pacific Gas and Electric Company referred to its billing as 'energy documents.' The shutdown at the General Motors plant in Framingham, Massachusetts, was labeled by the company as a 'volume-related production-schedule adjustment.' A recent publication claimed that jumping off a building could lead to 'sudden deceleration trauma.'" [1]

Other reasons for miscommunication are:
- Differing perceptions
- Having your words twisted and then used against you
- Differing value systems
- Perceived threat

Examples of Miscommunication

Where Did I Come From?

A little boy asked his Dad, "Where did I come from?" The dad, thinking the question was a little strange, decided to answer his inquiry. He began to talk about conception and birth. The boy appeared to be a little puzzled at his dad's answer, but remained silent. When Dad was done, he asked his boy, "Why did you ask your question, son?" The boy answered, "Johnny told me he was from Philadelphia, and I just wanted to know where I came from."

Misprints

Misprints can also lead to interesting miscommunication. Consider some of these humorous ones:

❐ Remember in prayer those who are sick of our church and community.
❐ Our next song is "Angels We Have Heard Get High"
❐ Thursday night—potluck supper. Prayers and medication will follow.
❐ Scouts are saving aluminum cans, bottles, and other items to be recycled. Proceeds will be used to cripple children.
❐ Apparently these cities even mined their own coins during the second century.
❐ Where did the Danites strop overnight as they were looking for land?
❐ A sweat aroma of worship that rises to Your throne.
❐ The senior choir invites any of those who enjoy sinning to join the choir.
❐ The church will host an evening of fine dining, superb entertainment, and gracious hostility.

Double Meanings

At times it is not misprints but double-meaning statements that can be humorous:

✛ At the evening service tonight, the sermon topic will be "What Is Hell?" Come early and listen to our choir practice.

✛ Next Thursday there will be tryouts for the choir. They need all the help they can get.

✛ Weight Watchers will meet at 7:00 p.m. Please use the large double doors at the side entrance.

✛ Low Self Esteem Support Group will meet Thursday at 7 p.m. Please use the back door.

✛ Jean will be leading a weight-management series Wednesday nights. She used the program herself and has been growing like crazy.

✛ Please place your donation in the envelope along with the deceased person(s) you want remembered.

✛ The peacemaking meeting scheduled for today has been canceled due to a conflict.

✛ The minister spoke briefly, much to the delight of his audience.

✛ During the absence of our minister, we enjoyed the rare privilege of hearing a good sermon when A.B. Doe supplied our pulpit.

✛ Ladies, don't forget the rummage sale. It's a chance to get rid of those things not worth keeping around the house. Don't forget your husbands.

Conclusion

We would hope that none of us have to experience the humiliation that David's men had to endure at the hands of King Hanun. That miscommunication resulted in the deaths of many innocent people. Regardless of misprints, misstatements, double meanings, unintentional gaffs, or mixed signals, we all must accept personal responsibility for our words. Jesus did say, "But I tell you that men will have to give account on the day of judgment for every careless word they have spoken" (Matt. 12:36). However, God is gracious and full of forgiveness to those who repent. We can be confident that the Righteous Judge will be just and merciful.

Thought for the Week

Fear is a very dangerous emotion which clouds our ability to communicate. It hinders and holds back the tongue when we speak, and it causes suspicion and misinterpretation when we listen. Ask God to help you conquer any fear you have.

Memory Verse for the Week

"Be wise in the way you act toward outsiders; make the most of every opportunity. Let your conversation be always full of grace, seasoned with salt, so that you may know how to answer everyone" (Col 4:5-6).

Endnote

1. Richard Saul Wurman, *Information Anxiety* (New York: Doubleday, 1998), p. 109.

Chapter 5

Mouth-o-Matic

When Words Are Painful

When Words Are Painful

Mouth-o-Matic

Chapter 5

Billy Graham reminds us,

Each of us has a tongue and a voice. These instruments of speech can be used destructively or employed constructively. I can use my tongue to slander, to gripe, to scold, to nag and to quarrel; or I can bring it under the control of God's Spirit and make it an instrument of blessing and praise. . . . Only God can control it, as we yield it to him.[1]

Consider this, "The rabbis used to say that the tongue is more dangerous than the hand: the hand kills only at a close range, while the tongue can kill at a great distance."[2]

The "Veg-a-Matic" was a popular kitchen utensil in the '80s. The slogan of this product was, "It slices and dices and makes julienne fries." The mouth is very similar to this utensil: It slices and dices and makes Julianne cry. How can *words* make Julianne cry? It is because words can be

> *persuasive* (Prov 7:21)
> *flattering* (Prov 28:23; 29:5; 1 Thess 2:5,6; Jude 16)
> *empty* (Isa 36:5; 2 Kgs 18:20)
> *seductive* (Prov 7:5,21)

a snare (Prov 6:2)
careless (Matt 12:36)
deceptive (Jer 7:4; Rom 3:13; 2 Cor 4:2)
insolent (Hos 7:16)
distorted (Jer 23:36)
killing (Hos 6:5)
scorching fire (Prov 16:27)
evil (Prov 17:4)
arrogant (Prov 17:7)
worthless (Jer 7:8)
harsh (Prov 15:1; Mal 3:13)
fearsome (Ezek 2:6)
hasty (Prov 29:20)
enticing (Col 2:4)
boastful (2 Pet 2:18)
malicious (3 John 10)
smooth (Prov 6:24; 7:21)
angry (2 Cor 12:20; Col 3:8)
arrogant boasting (2 Tim 3:2; Jas 4:16)
godless chatter (1 Tim 6:20; 2 Tim 2:16)

Words can be rude, insensitive, cruel, cold, mean, dishonoring, vicious, antagonizing, irritating, and calculating. There may be more negative words than positive in most people's vocabularies. Proverbs 15:2 explains that ". . . the mouth of fools gushes folly." Proverbs 15:28 states, ". . . but the mouth of the wicked gushes evil." Proverbs 12:23, ". . . but the heart of fools blurts out folly."

A warning must be given here: words can ruin relationships and reputations! They can devastate the reputation and relationship of both the speaker and listener. Words can be **W**eapons **o**f **R**epeated **D**estruction. Consider the woman whose husband tells her after she has lost thirty pounds that he hasn't noticed; these words can wound or destroy. The ex-wife whose husband always put her down is going to struggle with her second husband when he compliments what the first husband ridiculed. The ex-husband whose wife insulted what he did for a living and how much money he made will struggle with his second wife when she compliments what the first wife insulted. They have made criticism normal.

Compliments can then be seen as remarks made with an ulterior motive. They can be interpreted as punishment, blackmail, or simple flattery. *Insincere* compliments hurt relationships.

Fruit of Our Lips

The Bible teaches that every word produces a fruit or by-product (Prov 12:14; 13:2; 18:20-21). What can words do, be, or bring? Old Testament authors wrote that the tongue can

> *slander* (Prov 10:18)
> *nourish* (Prov 10:21)
> *destroy* (Prov 11:9,11)
> *trap or help* (Prov 12:13)
> *reward* (Prov 12:14)
> *pierce and heal* (Prov 12:18)
> *guard or ruin* (Prov 13:3)
> *promote instruction* (Prov 16:21)
> be *persuasive* (Prov 7:21)
> *right* (Prov 8:6; 23:16; Eccl 12:10)
> *worthy* (Prov 8:6)
> *fitting or perverse* (Prov 10:32)
> *truthful or lying* (Prov 12:22; 14:5)
> *healing or crushing* (Prov 15:4; 16:24; Job 19:2)
> *undoing and a snare* (Prov 18:7)
> *filling and satisfying* (Prov 18:20)
> *life and death* (Prov 18:21)
> *gracious* (Prov 22:11)
> *a deep pit* (Prov 22:14)

> *honest* (Prov 24:26)
> *reassuring and kind* (Gen 50:21)
> *trustworthy* (2 Sam 7:28)
> *loving* (John 19:26-27)
> *sound* (Titus 2:8)
> bring *life or violence* (Prov 10:11)
> *wisdom* (Prov 10:13,31)
> *revenge or rescue* (Prov 12:6)
> *good things and violence* (Prov 13:2)
> *strife and beating* (Prov 18:6)
> *punishment, bondage, and perishing* (Prov 19:5,9)
> *goodwill and assurance* (Esth 9:30)
> cause *beating or protection* (Prov 14:3)
> produce *knowledge or folly* (Prov 15:2,7; 20:15)

Can you see the potential good or harm in any and every spoken word?

Solomon's Comments on the Injuring, Harmful Tongue

Proverbs discusses in greater detail how the tongue can cause injury.

Proverbs 11:9, "With his mouth the godless destroys his neighbor, but through knowledge the righteous escape." The mouth can destroy by what it says, but it can also destroy by what it does not say.

Proverbs 12:6, "The words of the wicked lie in wait for blood, but the speech of the upright rescues them." By "lie in wait for blood" revenge and plotting harm are obvious. Mean words look for the "best" time to be spoken. The best time is when they can do the most damage and infliction of pain. This is bitter, evil, wicked communication.

Proverbs 12:18, "Reckless words pierce like a sword, but the tongue of the wise brings healing." Reckless words like reckless drivers can destroy property and life. These words are out of control. When the tongue is out of control, it is the speaker who loses control. Many can die emotionally from this form of communication.

Proverbs 13:3, "He who guards his lips guards his life, but he who speaks rashly will come to ruin." "Rash" means without thinking through the possible consequences. Look what Solomon wrote in Proverbs 18:1-4, "An unfriendly man pursues selfish ends; he defies all sound judgment. A fool finds no pleasure in understanding but delights in airing his own opinions. When wickedness comes, so does contempt, and with shame comes disgrace. The words of a man's mouth are deep waters, but the fountain of wisdom is a bubbling brook."

Proverbs 15:4, "The tongue that brings healing is a tree of life, but a deceitful tongue crushes the spirit." The tongue can crush the spirit and soul. Solomon wrote, "A happy heart makes the face cheerful, but heartache crushes the spirit" (Prov 15:13). He also wrote, "A cheerful heart is good medicine, but a crushed spirit dries up the bones" (Prov 17:22).

Proverbs 15:28, "The heart of the righteous weighs its answers, but the mouth of the wicked gushes evil." Words can be very evil. The word "evil" occurs 464 times in the NIV translation of the Bible.

Proverbs 18:6-8, "A fool's lips bring him strife, and his mouth invites a beating. A fool's mouth is his undoing, and his lips are a snare to his soul. The words of a gossip are like choice morsels; they go down to a man's inmost parts." Gossip is something that people like to hear. It is like a tasty snack. Listening to gossip is listening to evil (Prov 17:4). I found a great quote from an unknown source, "A gossip is a person who jumps to a conclusion, takes people at deface value, and knows how to add to and to."[3]

The Psalms and the Mouth-o-Matic

"You speak continually against your brother and slander your own mother's son" (Psalm 50:20). Continually means continually; this is the Mouth-o-Matic.

"My companion attacks his friends; he violates his covenant. His speech is smooth as butter, yet war is in his heart; his words are more soothing than oil, yet they are drawn swords" (Ps 55:20-21). Speech can soothe and yet destroy — this is hypocrisy, or being two-faced. Maybe even forked tongued?

David continues, "I am in the midst of lions; I lie among ravenous beasts — men whose teeth are spears and arrows, whose tongues are sharp swords" (Ps 57:4). David had to face a lot of criticism from his political foes. He constantly experienced the damaging effects of his enemies' critical tongues.

"They sharpen their tongues like swords and aim their words like deadly arrows" (Ps 64:3). Deadly words are often sharpened by practice. They are learned by watching and listening to others communicate. These words are premeditated to harm. They pierce the heart and soul and can do irreparable damage.

Sticks and Stones

One of the more humorous lies I heard while growing up was: "Sticks and stones may break my bones, but words will never hurt me." Sticks and stones can do a lot of damage. They are able to physically injure people. Words, however, can be just as harmful and are able to permanently ruin relationships. Consider some of the verbal sticks and stones that we hurl at one another.

> I wish you were never born.
> I have been praying a curse on everything you do.
> I will be glad when you graduate and leave home.
> Children are to be seen and not heard.
> If you don't stop crying, I'll give you a reason to cry.
> Use your head for more than just a hat rack.
> That's dumb.
> I wish you would grow up.
> I wish I had parents like Billy's; they are nice.
> I hate you.
> I wish you were a boy instead of a girl.
> I hope that when you grow up and have kids, you have
>   one just like you.
> I disown you as my son.
> You're only a housewife.
> I am the only one who works and earns money in this
>   home.
> I can spend my money any way I'd like.

Physical assaults have a visible manifestation; words, though, cause invisible harm. Injuries caused by words can take a longer time to heal than physical injuries. Sometimes they may not heal at all. Permanent damage from words is not uncommon.

The Source of Criticism

When we experience insults and criticism, we must consider the source of those words. Consider these critical remarks from supposed "experts."

The manager of the Cleveland Indians, Tris Speaker, said of Babe Ruth: "He made a great mistake when he gave up pitching. Working once a week, he might have lasted a long time and become a great star."

Jim Denny, manager of the Grand Ole Opry, fired Elvis Presley after a 1954 performance and said, "You ain't goin' nowhere, son. You ought to go back to drivin' a truck."

The president of Decca Records said of the Beatles in 1962, "We don't like the sound. Groups of guitars are on the way out." Alan Livingston, president of Capital Records, on the verge of the Beatles' first U.S. tour in 1964, said, "We don't think they'll do anything in this market."[4]

Before we let a critical remark hurt us, we need to consider whether the speaker has any basis for knowing what he is talking about.

Parents, siblings, spouses, friends, coworkers, and neighbors can speak the most critical, harmful words that can have the greatest negative effect. When criticized by a total stranger, most people can easily blow it off. But when people we respect or love criticize us, the words make a deeper impact. Words can take root and "stick" in our memories for years and be replayed for a whole lifetime.

The Power of the Spoken Word to Hurt or Heal

The dangers with any spoken word include two different aspects. They are *irrevocable* by the speaker and *unforgettable* by the listener! Even saying "I'm sorry" does not take away the impact of the words. The sad fact is our mouth can create lots of harm and injury that may possibly never be repaired. In the heat of the moment the tongue can be like a hurricane—destroying anything in its path.

The length of a statement is not important. Damage or healing can occur with very few words. Here are some of the most important *healing* statements I think people can say

The most important *one-word* statements: "Neat." "Cool." "Thanks."

The most important *two-word* statement: "Thank you!"

The most important *three-word* statements: "I love you!" "I forgive you!" "I was wrong!"

The most important *four-word* statement: "I am very sorry."

The most important *five-word* statement: "I appreciate what you did."

The most important *six-word* statements: "Please forgive me for hurting you." "I am glad I married you." "I am glad you're my child." "You are a gift to me."

The most important *seven-word* statement: "I'm proud of who you have become."

The most important *eight-word* statement: "I'm glad God gave you to us both."

The most important *nine-word* statement: "Marrying you was the best thing I ever did."

The most important *ten-word* statement: "Taking you to heaven with me is my utmost mission."

How often do you make the above statements? What makes them difficult to say? How can these statements become less difficult to say? How often do you hear these statements? Are these statements the greatest words you've never heard? Make a change and add them to your frequent vocabulary!

These words also must be accompanied by actions or they mean nothing. First John 3:18 says we must love with action and truth, not with word and tongue. What are some of the actions that are needed to back up these words?

The Psalms and the Healing Effects of Words

Psalm 37:30, "The mouth of the righteous man utters wisdom, and his tongue speaks what is just." The mouth can speak wisdom and be just. When we choose our words carefully, we will speak wise words that will greatly benefit those around us.

Psalm 39:1, "I said, 'I will watch my ways and keep my tongue from sin; I will put a muzzle on my mouth as long as the wicked are in my presence.'" The person puts the muzzle on himself. This is part of self-control, the last characteristic of the fruit of the Spirit (Gal 5:22-23). The way to keep the tongue from sinning comes from self-control and choices. People will be only as pure and holy as they choose to be. All behavior and every spoken word is by choice!

Psalm 40:3, "He put a new song in my mouth, a hymn of praise to our God. Many will see and fear and put their trust in the LORD." This new song can get into a person's mouth only when it enters the heart. This begins with the prayer found in Psalm 19:14, "May the words of my mouth and the meditation of my heart be pleasing in your sight, O LORD, my Rock and my Redeemer."

Psalm 51:15, "O Lord, open my lips, and my mouth will declare your praise." David wanted God to speak through him. What a great prayer! We should all desire God's words and godly speech to flow from our lips.

Psalm 71:8, "My mouth is filled with your praise, declaring your splendor all day long." If the mouth can be filled with praise, it can also be empty of it. This once again is a person's choice. Philippians 4:8 teaches the best thought pattern the heart can have in order for it to be filled with praise, "Finally, brothers, whatever is true, whatever is noble, whatever is right, whatever is pure, whatever is lovely, whatever is admirable—if anything is excellent or praiseworthy—think about such things."

Psalm 71:15, "My mouth will tell of your righteousness, of your salvation all day long, though I know not its measure." Constant reassurance of salvation can build self-esteem as well as produce a pleasant disposition.

Psalm 106:1-5, "Praise the LORD. Give thanks to the LORD, for he is good; his love endures forever. Who can proclaim the mighty acts of the LORD or fully declare his praise? Blessed are they who maintain justice, who constantly do what is right. Remember me, O LORD, when you show favor to your people, come to my aid when you save them, that I may enjoy the prosperity of your chosen ones, that I may share in the joy of your nation and join your inheritance in giving praise." Praise for who God is will prepare a dwelling place for him. Respect and love for his people will perpetuate a dwelling place for us during our pilgrimage on earth.

Psalm 141:3, "Set a guard over my mouth, O LORD; keep watch over the door of my lips." This guard is set by prayer and used through self-control. The mouth and heart should be guarded because they are vulnerable to sin and can cause much damage.

Psalm 145:21, "My mouth will speak in praise of the LORD. Let every creature praise his holy name for ever and ever." All creatures praise God by what they do (Ps 19:1-2).

Conclusion

With positive biblical input, your Mouth-o-Matic can automatically speak words of comfort, love, and healing. We know from Hebrews that the Old Testament writers used words for our instruction (Heb 1–3). From Paul's letter to the

Philippians we know that we can redirect our thinking so that our output will be pleasing to the Lord Jesus (Phil 4:8,9). The choice is ours. Will our words be the sticks and stones of verbal assault or will they be gems and balm for those around us?

Thoughts for the Week

Every question is not a challenge or threat to integrity, professionalism, competency, or character. If they are perceived that way, communication breaks down.

I will let you say anything to your spouse you want, any way you want, under one condition: that I can say the same thing to him or her and you won't get mad at me! It hurts more when the words come from you! Words can do permanent damage!

Memory Verses for the Week

"May the words of my mouth and the meditation of my heart be pleasing in your sight, O LORD, my Rock and my Redeemer" (Ps 19:14).

"May the LORD cut off all flattering lips and every boastful tongue that says, 'We will triumph with our tongues; we own our lips—who is our master?'" (Ps 12:3-4).

Endnotes

1. Cited in Max Lucado, *Life Lessons with Max Lucado Book of James* (Dallas, TX: Word, 1996), p. 52.

2. Ken Durham, *Speaking from the Heart: Richer Relationships through Communication* (Ft. Worth: Sweet, 1986), p. 20.

3. Vern McLellan, *Quips, Quotes and Quests* (Eugene, OR: Harvest House, 1982), p. 61.

4. Parrott, *High-Maintenance*, p. 10.

Chapter 6

I'm Beginning to Look like an Israelite

Champion Gripers

The Children of Israel did not have a corner on complaining. Did you know that October 15 is National Grouch Day? Only in America would we have a day devoted to grouching. We complain about many things. If I were to write them all, this book could not hold them. We complain about everything from having to wait in line at the fast food drive-through, to the amount of pay we receive. We complain as people around the world lose their belongings to floods and earthquakes. They have lost the little they had while we complain that we don't have more!

Training for Complaining

We learn to complain at a very young age. Many times children could compete with the best complaining adults. The top ten things children complain about (not necessarily in order) are

Getting up early for school ("I'm tired.")
Having to go to bed ("I'm not tired.")

What they eat ("Do we have to eat that again? We had that last week.")

Chores that have to be done ("You never make Billy do that around the house.")

Doing homework ("This teacher gives us too much homework.")

Having to go to school ("I don't feel like going to school today.")

Cleaning up after themselves ("But I set the table.")

Where to go to eat ("I don't want to go there; we went there last week.")

What kind of clothing and shoes they have to wear ("If I don't wear these $95.00 shoes, all the kids will make fun of me. I will have no friends and be uncool.")

Having to bathe/personal hygiene ("I took a shower yesterday; why do I have to take one today? I hate brushing my teeth and combing my hair.")

What we complain about having to do, 95% of the world would like to have. Our children complain because they don't want to go to a particular restaurant while people in the world are starving. We have turned complaining into a fine art. Several examples from modern life illustrate this point.

"Back to Rationing for Daughter"

When she got fed up with the frequent complaints of her 14-year-old daughter, Janet, at the dining table, Mrs. Fay Young decided to do something about it.

She went to the library to research what she as a girl had eaten during the London blitz in the Second World War. Then she put daughter Janet on the same diet—a week's ration of 14 ounces of meat, 3 eggs, 3 pounds of potatoes, and 2 ounces of cheese. Sunday dinner was bread and butter and a hard-boiled egg.

"It was a good lesson," Janet decided. "I'll never complain again."[1]

"Going to the Complaint Department"

Entering a department store, a little old lady was startled when a band began to play and a dignified executive pinned an orchid on her dress and handed her a crisp hundred-dollar bill. She was the store's millionth customer. Television cameras were focused on her and reporters began interviewing.

"Tell me," one asked, "just what did you come here for today?"

The lady hesitated for a minute, then answered, "I'm on my way to the Complaint Department."[2]

"Complainers Live Longer?"

A recent medical survey reveals that chronic complainers live longer than people who are always sweet and serene. It claims that their cantankerous spirit gives them a purpose for living. Each morning they get up with a fresh challenge to see how many things they can find to grumble about, and they derive great satisfaction from making others miserable.

"I question whether those who complain actually do outlive those who don't. Maybe it just seems that way to everybody around them" — Herbert Vander Lugt.[3]

And the Award Goes to . . .

Can you name the worst complainers, grumblers and whiners in Scripture? The Israelites exiting from Egypt! These guys could complain and grumble like no one else found in Scripture. Consider several passages that discuss their continual complaining.

Exodus 16:7, "and in the morning you will see the glory of the LORD, because he has heard your grumbling against him. Who are we, that you should grumble against us?"

Numbers 14:26-27, "The LORD said to Moses and Aaron, 'How long will this wicked community grumble against me? I have heard the complaints of these grumbling Israelites.'"

Numbers 14:36, "So the men Moses had sent to explore the land, who returned and made the whole community grumble against him by spreading a bad report about it—"

Numbers 16:11, "It is against the LORD that you and all your followers have banded together. Who is Aaron that you should grumble against him?"

Numbers 11:1-20 tells us a lot about their bad habit!

Now the people complained about their *hardships* in the hearing of the LORD, and when he heard them his anger was aroused. . . .

The *rabble* with them began to *crave other food*, and again the Israelites started wailing and said, "*If only we had meat to eat! We remember the fish we ate in Egypt at no cost—also the cucumbers, melons, leeks, onions and garlic.* But now we have lost our appetite; we never see anything but this manna!"

. . . .

Moses heard the people of every family *wailing,* each at the entrance to his tent. The LORD *became exceedingly angry,* and Moses was troubled. . . . (emphases added).

God was angry about this grumbling and complaining (Num 11:10). Moses was troubled (11:10). God created a plague that he inflicted on the people because of their complaining (Num 11:33). I think this stopped them from ever again complaining about the food they were eating. What a graphic picture of how God deals with complaining!

The Selective Memory of the Israelites

Those Israelites, who were children when God rescued them from slavery, needed to be reminded of all God had done for them. God did not want them to forget and thus fall into the trap of complaining and bitterness.

"Remember that you were slaves in Egypt and that the LORD your God brought you out of there with a mighty hand and an outstretched arm. Therefore the LORD your God has commanded you to observe the Sabbath day" (Deut 5:15).

"Remember that you were slaves in Egypt and the LORD your God redeemed you. That is why I give you this command today" (Deut 15:15).

"I am the LORD your God, who brought you out of Egypt so that you would no longer be slaves to the Egyptians; I broke the bars of your yoke and enabled you to walk with heads held high" (Lev 26:13).

It seems they had forgotten the Promised Land. They had also forgotten the One who had made the promise. How could they forget the yokes and bars that God removed from them? Was this a case of "what have you done for me lately?" Did they forget the plagues and God's presence with them? Does this remind you of your own forgetfulness and tendency to complain? I see myself as an Israelite sometimes. Does the complaining theme of this chapter hit too close to home for you as well?

What did they remember? "We remember the fish we ate in Egypt at no cost—also the cucumbers, melons, leeks, onions and garlic" (Num 11:5). Of all things to remember, the food. They must have had some wonderful dining experiences on the banks of the Nile. It's almost like they made the 400 years in Egyptian paradise a family vacation.

Other Expert Complainers in the Bible

Job spends several chapters of his narrative complaining about the treatment he has received from God. After the ruin of his family and property, Job feels he is justified in complaining out of the "anguish" of his spirit (Job 7:11).

In Genesis 21:25 we are told of Abraham's complaining, "Then Abraham complained to Abimelech about a well of water that Abimelech's servants had seized."

The Pharisees and teachers of the law complained to Jesus about the people with whom he ate—tax collectors and "sinners" (Luke 5:30). They also complained about Jesus' lack of fasting (Luke 5:33). How did Jesus respond to these inquiries? "Jesus answered them, 'It is not the healthy who need a doctor, but the sick. I have not come to call the righteous, but sinners to repentance'" (Luke 5:31-32). "Jesus answered, 'Can you make the guests of the bridegroom fast while he is with them? But the time will come when the bridegroom will be taken from them; in those days they will fast'" (Luke 5:34-35).

We can also see that the early church was not exempt from occasional bouts of complaining. The Grecian Jews complained, "In those days when the number of disciples was increasing, the Grecian Jews among them complained against the Hebraic Jews because their widows were being overlooked in the daily distribution of food" (Acts 6:1). Their complaint brought about the development of assigning deacons in the church (Acts 6:2-6).

God's Attitude toward Complaining

Several verses in the Bible teach what we should do or not do when it comes to arguing, grumbling, and complaining. "And do not grumble, as some of them did—and were killed by the destroying angel" (1 Cor 10:10). Paul wrote in Philippians 2:14, "Do everything without complaining or arguing." What does the word "everything" mean? James wrote about grumbling, "Don't grumble against each other, brothers, or you will be judged. The Judge is standing at the door!" (Jas 5:9).

In the parable of the workers in the vineyard (Matt 20:1-16), the workers complained about unfair pay. Were they treated unfairly? Was the treatment they were calling unfair, actually unfair?

The Antidote to Complaining

Gratitude can help control complaining. I want to close this chapter with a prayer broadcast on Christian radio:

Even though I clutch my blanket and growl when the alarm rings, thank you, Lord, that I can hear. There are many who are deaf.

Even though I keep my eyes closed against the morning light as long as possible, thank you, Lord, that I can see. Many are blind.

Even though I huddle in my bed and put off rising, thank you, Lord, that I have the strength to rise. There are many who are bedridden.

Even though the first hour of my day is hectic, when socks are lost, toast is burned and tempers are short, and my children are so loud, thank you, Lord, for my family. There are many who are lonely.

Even though our breakfast table never looks like the pictures in the magazines and the menu is at times unbalanced, thank you, Lord, for the food we have. There are many who are hungry.

Even though the routine of my job is often monotonous, thank you, Lord, for the opportunity to work. There are many who are jobless.

Even though I grumble and bemoan my fate from day to day and wish my circumstances were not so modest, thank you, Lord, for life.[4]

Conclusion

It takes self-discipline and self-control to stop complaining. Self-control and self-discipline are probably two of the least talked about spiritual gifts. They are also two of the least used spiritual gifts. We must see our spirit of complaining as a poor witness to those around us. If I want my kids to stop complaining, then I have to stop comlaining! If I want my kids to be servants, then I have to be a servant!

Thoughts for the Week

Complaining about what God gives us in life is telling God we could do a better job with our life than he is currently doing.

Mary Poppins said, "Enough is as good as a feast."[5] There are people though who never get enough. There are people who are never content. This possibly is one of Satan's most common attacks.

Memory Verse for the Week

"Though you probe my heart and examine me at night, though you test me, you will find nothing; I have resolved that my mouth will not sin" (Ps 17:3).

Endnotes

1. Tan, *Encyclopedia of 7,700 Illustrations*, pp. 255-256.
2. Ibid., p. 256.
3. Ibid.
4. From Phil Reaser, WBCL Radio, Fort Wayne, IN.
5. *Mary Poppins*, The Walt Disney Company, MCMLXIV

Chapter 7

Unwholesome Kinds of Communication

Unwholesome Kinds of Communication

Chapter 7

Tim LaHaye wrote:

> Lack of communication is almost always a problem for couples who come to me for marriage counseling. If it is not lack of communication, it is wrong communication. Communicating under pressure of anger and shouting at the top of one's voice is the wrong approach. This is communication that could well be omitted in every marriage. Problems and differences in marriage are not dangerous—not being able to communicate the differences, or problem areas, is dangerous. As long as two people can keep the lines of communication open and freely express their feelings, differences can be resolved.[1]

What a great lesson for all of us!

In this chapter we will be discussing many forms of communication that are unwholesome. All of these forms are dangerous and potentially deadly to relationships. These unwholesome communication patterns are some of the flaming arrows of the evil one (Eph 6:16). These forms need to be extinguished!

Get your Bibles out because we are going to read some Scriptures and then ask some questions about the communication going on in each passage. We will ask more questions than we answer — have fun thinking!

New Testament Greek Terms

In looking up Greek words in the New Testament I found several that deal with negative types of communication. This is by no means a comprehensive list but will help us get a picture of the type of communication God abhors.

oneidizo — to reproach; to defame, disparage, to rail, revile, assail with abusive words (Matt 5:11; 27:44; Mark 15:32; Luke 6:22; Rom 15:3)[2]

blasphemeo — to speak profanely; to hurt the reputation or smite with reports or words; speak evil of, slander (Mark 3:28; 15:29; Luke 23:39; Acts 18:6; 19:37; 26:11)[3]

chleuazo — to mock, scoff, deride with words (Acts 2:13; 17:32)[4]

empaizo — to play; to sport with or against someone; to deride, mock, or scoff at (Matt 27:29,31; Mark 10:34; 15:20; Luke 14:29; 22:63; 23:36)[5]

mukterizo — to turn up one's nose in scorn and hence to mock (Gal 6:7)[6]

katagelao — to laugh at; to scorn, deride, ridicule (Matt 9:24; Mark 5:40; Luke 8:53)[7]

hubrizo — to injure, insult, reproach; to treat shamefully, injure, abuse (Matt 22:6; Luke 18:32; Acts 14:5; 1 Thess 2:2)[8]

anathematizo — to utterly curse (Mark 14:71; Acts 23:12, 14,21)[9]

kakologeo — to speak evil (Matt 15:4; Mark 7:10)[10]

aischrologia — to be foul-mouthed; filthy, improper, vile conversation (Col 3:8)[11]

diaballo — to falsely accuse (Luke 16:1)[12]

sukophanteo — to falsely accuse; to inform against; to totally defraud (Luke 3:14; 19:8)[13]

kategoreo — to speak openly against; to condemn or accuse, mainly in a legal sense (Matt 12:10; Mark 3:2; 15:3; Luke 11:54; 23:2,10; John 5:45; 8:6; Acts 22:30; 24:2,8,19; 25:5,11; 28:19; Rom 2:15; Rev 12:10)[14]

Unhealthy Communication Patterns

1. "Sink hole—quick sand communication": The longer you talk about a topic the lower you go. There is a point of no return in this type of communication.

2. "People who don't say what they mean": There is an old song titled "Games People Play." One of the lines says, "Never meaning what they say, never saying what they mean."

3. "Jugular communication": This is a quick-kill communication pattern I know people who can get to the jugular of others faster than surgeons during an operation! These people bring up painful past experiences of others just to harm them.

4. "Pre-statements communication": These statements can put a person on the defensive: "I don't mean to hurt you, but . . . ." "We need to talk." "There is something I need to tell you." These statements only introduce the statement we *really* want to make. We are hoping the pre-statement will soften the blow, but the opposite usually occurs.

5. "Cold, heartless, and apathetic communication": These people do not meet needs or care about the person with whom they communicate. The chief priests and elders were skilled at this form of communication. Consider their response that prompted Judas's suicide (Matt 27:4-5). They could not have been more heartless and cold. Instead of their removing and relieving guilt, they only heaped it on when

they told him, "That's your responsibility." Remember this was coming from the religious leaders! What Judas expected and what he received were two different things. They should have been ashamed at their response to him!

6. "*Readers' Digest/Dragnet* communication": "Just the facts, ma'am." These people hate long stories. They want to "cut to the chase." The briefer the better with them. Long stories lull them to sleep. Unfortunately, they cut the speaker when they cut their time with him.

7. "Repeated questioners": For this type of speaker an answer prompts more questions. This pattern prompts the nonquestion speaker to run away because he does not know how to answer, and he knows that an answer will only prompt more questions. He often becomes frustrated and will avoid this type of speaker.

8. "*But* speakers": These types of speakers will make a statement and then add the word "but" which means "Forget what I said before the word 'but.'" The truth of "but" statements are found after the word "but," not before. Consider this statement and look at how adding the word "but" changes the whole meaning.

"I love your hair."

"I love your hair, *but* . . . ."

Do you see the difference in these two statements?

9. "Sidewalk communicators": These people ask questions of others as people walk toward them. By the time the answer is given, this person is already beyond them and on their way. These people ask questions without really wanting to listen to the answer.

10. "Tangent speakers": These people start with one story, and in the middle of it they talk about another story that is remotely connected (usually in their own mind) to the first story. These people are the *War and Peace* communicators. They communicate with long, drawn out diatribes. They can take what should be a five-minute conversation

and make it a lifetime, or at least it can seem like it. People can hate asking questions of these people.

Negative Styles of Communication

If edification is the only prescribed form of communication endorsed in the Bible, how many styles of communication does the Bible say we should not have? Consider the following:

☆ **Liars, Deceivers**

The Bible teaches that people should not lie (Ps 5:6; Exod 20:16; 23:1; Lev 19:11). What are the consequences when people catch you in a lie? What do you lose when you are caught in a lie? Respect from others.

Many liars are found in the Bible. The most notorious one is Satan (John 8:44; Gen 3:4-5; Matt 4:8-9). A few others would be Adam and Eve (Gen 3:12,13), Cain (Gen 4:9), Abraham (Gen 12:11-19; 20:2), Sarah (Gen 18:15; 20:5,16), Isaac (Gen 26:7-10), Jacob's sons (Gen 34), Joseph's brothers (Gen 37:29-35), Potiphar's wife (Gen 39:14-17), and Aaron (Exod 32:1-24).

1. What was the penalty for lying spelled out in Deuteronomy 19:16-20?
2. What are the things that God hates that are found in Proverbs 6:16-19?
3. What does Proverbs 14:5 mean when it refers to one who "pours out lies"?
4. Why is it better to be a poor man than a liar (Prov 19:22)?
5. What are the consequences of swearing falsely in Zechariah 5:3,4?
6. What were the two things John the Baptist said not to do (Luke 3:14)? What did he say people should do?

7. Can liars be trusted? What happens when they are actually telling the truth? Are there actually "white lies"?
8. Why do liars need good memories (Prov 21:6)? How would not remembering the lie told be a snare?

Psalm 58:3 states, "Even from birth the wicked go astray; from the womb they are wayward and speak lies." The habit of lying can develop at a young age. What is Solomon attributing the lying to in this verse? "A lying tongue hates those it hurts, and a flattering mouth works ruin" (Prov 26:28). A couple of other reasons people lie are to get out of trouble or to build self-esteem.

Solomon compares lying to weapons, "Like a club or a sword or a sharp arrow is the man who gives false testimony against his neighbor" (Prov 25:18). According to Proverbs 15:4, deceit (another word for lie) can crush us. "The tongue that brings healing is a tree of life, but a deceitful tongue crushes the spirit."

Two Lying Examples

The prevalence of lying in today's world is no different than in biblical times. It is endorsed and even recommended but is never without its consequences. Consider these two stories.

First, Chevy Chase has come a long way since his days at *Saturday Night Live*—he's received an honorary degree from his alma mater and given a commencement address. Chase, a 1968 graduate of Bard College, was honored at the 700-student college 90 miles north of New York City.

His words of wisdom for the class of 1990: "Avoid fatty foods. Avoid smoking, drugs, Bensonhurst, the Gaza Strip, bungee jumping, humorless people, bad music, fashion, weight training and hair-care products. Oh, and one more thing. Never tell the truth. Embellish, patronize, pander, use hyperbole, braggadocio—modify, but never actually tell the truth."

His remarks were well received by the students.[15]

Chevy Chase's profound wisdom consists of telling students to lie. The irony is that every word spoken has consequences. Consider what happened to Tim Johnson because of his lies.

> Dunedin, Florida—The lies Tim Johnson told about his Marine service in Vietnam cost him the trust of his team. Now, it's cost him his job.
>
> Johnson never saw combat, but supposedly made up stories—including shooting a young girl—to inspire the team. He taught mortar training to recruits going to Vietnam, yet never served there. The truth was revealed last year, causing conflicts with several players and pitching coach Mel Queen. Johnson apologized to the club at camp last month, trying to put behind him a winter full of turmoil.
>
> But with the Blue Jays at 3-12, and just a few days after former Toronto player Ed Sprague called Johnson a "liar" and a "backstabber," General Manager Gord Ash had seen enough. Johnson was fired at 1 a.m. after a loss to the Yankees.[16]

☆ Sarcastic People

Can these people be trusted in what they say? In Proverbs 26:18-19 Solomon compares this person to "a madman shooting firebrands or deadly arrows" and "a man who deceives his neighbor and says, 'I was only joking!'" What does "I was just joking" mean?

☆ Those Who Insult and Show Disrespect

One of my favorite stories in the Bible is that of youths insulting Elisha about his chrome dome. They called him "baldhead" (2 Kgs 2:23-25). This was highly insulting and disrespectful. Answer these:

1. What was Elisha's response to these disrespectful children (2 Kgs 2:24)?
2. Why do people call others names? Is name-calling disrespectful?

3. How does this relate to Lamentations 5:12 and 1 Peter 2:17?

☆ Those Who Turn Cold Shoulders and Wage Cold Wars

Terry Hekker said, "The only inhumane weapon that should be outlawed by international convention is silence. Silence is very effective but inordinately cruel. Words wound but silence tears you apart."[17] This is not the same type of silence discussed in chapter 9. This silence is used for the purpose of shutting people out. It makes ice look warm.

1. According to Proverbs 28:9 what is the consequence of "turning a deaf ear"? What is the fulfillment of the law stated in Romans 13:10?
2. How does Solomon describe cold people in Proverbs 25:14? Why did this person not give the gift he could have? Is this cruel and wicked communication?
3. Why did Absalom not talk to Amnon (2 Sam 13:1-15)? What was the emotion that prompted this lack of communication (2 Sam 13:22)? What was the end result to this cold-war conflict (2 Sam 13:39)?

Warning: These people tend to be indifferent to needs of others. They also tend to be impersonal, uninterested, silent, emotionally withdrawn, and oblivious to other people's hurts and tears. This is a highly destructive communication pattern and should be changed as quickly as possible! The damage this pattern of communication can cause is limitless.

☆ Those Who Gossip, Accuse Falsely, and Slander

"Gossip has the potential to damage and destroy two of our most precious personal possessions: our relationships and our reputation."[18]

1. What does Solomon call a slanderer in Proverbs 10:18?
2. What does Solomon mean in Proverbs 18:8? How is

gossip like food? Is gossip like a "juicy piece of meat" and "sweet candy"?

3. What does a gossip do according to Proverbs 20:19? What is the warning found in this passage? Why should we follow this warning?

4. How did Paul handle slander according to 1 Corinthians 4:13?

5. According to Paul in Ephesians 4:31, what did Paul want the people to get rid of? How many of these things would influence communication?

6. What was Paul's instruction to Titus to be taught to the people according to Titus 3:1-2?

7. How does God describe the wicked (Ps 50:16-20)?

8. According to Proverbs 16:28 what is the consequence of gossip?

9. What does Paul link to gossip in 1 Timothy 5:13? Why do these people talk about their friends when they are not around? What do gossips do when they are confronted? Are you really open with your feelings and ideas to people like this?

10. According to Jesus what is the result of a person having false things said about him because he is a Christian (Matthew 5:11)?

11. According to Matthew 27:12-14 what did Jesus do when he was accused by the chief priests and elders? What does this teach about answering slander?

12. In 1 Peter 3:15-16 what is the benefit of a clear conscience?

13. What does James 4:11 teach about slander? What is the definition of slander in this passage?

☆ **Naggers and Prodders**

1. What are the consequences found in Judges 16:16 about nagging? What was Delilah repeatedly reminding Samson of in this story? Why do people nag?

Does nagging motivate? What three-word phrase is linked with nagging in this verse? (See also Prov 10:19.)

2. Did Job feel nagged by his friends (Job 19:3)? The King James Version uses the word "press" — what would that mean? How does this relate to Luke 11:5-8? Does nagging create rebellion? Why? What is the "naggee" thinking as he/she is being nagged? Is it, "If you would quit nagging, I would do what you ask"? The nagger is thinking, "I did ask and it wasn't done, so this is my only way of getting things done." Can you see how these ideas oppose each other and create conflict?

3. How does this relate to Luke 18:1-6? Are we supposed to nag and *press* God with our communication (prayers)?

4. Do children seek to wear down their parents by nagging? Does it work? How often? Could kids nag to create parental frustrations with the hope that the parents will give in? Children must realize the word "no" is a complete sentence.

5. Did the adulterous woman nag and press in Proverbs 7:11-27? What was the outcome?

☆ **Grumblers, Those Who Criticize, and Complainers**
1. What does Philippians 2:14 say people should not do?

2. What is a consequence of grumbling found in James 5:9?

3. What did Paul say had happened to a grumbler in 1 Corinthians 10:10? Why did Paul write about this according to 1 Corinthians 10:11?

4. Can you think of people in the Bible who complained or grumbled? Here is a *short* list:

> Cain (Gen 4:13-14)
> Rachel (Gen 30:1)

Moses (Exod 5:22-23)
Israelites (Exod 16:8)
Korah (Num 16:8-11)
David (2 Sam 6:8; Ps 35:17; 116:10-11)
Elijah (1 Kgs 19:4,10)
Job (Job 30:21-31)
Asaph (Ps 73:3)
Prodigals (Prov 19:3)
Solomon (Eccl 2:17-18)
Hezekiah (Isa 38:10-18)
Jeremiah (Jer 20:7)
Jonah (Jonah 4:1-3)
Martha (Luke 10:40)
Jews about Jesus (John 6:41-43,52)
Grecian Jews to the Apostles (Acts 6:1)
Godless men (Jude 16)

Do you ask complainers for help? If you do it once, do you do it again?

Gary Smalley shares two ways a husband can hurt his wife:

1. He frequently criticizes her.
2. He doesn't pay attention to her words or ideas.[19]

He continues,

It's extremely important that you never ridicule or belittle any of your husband's attempts to comfort you. Even when his attempts are inadequate, rather than calling attention to his failure, praise him for anything positive in his actions. (Even the attempt itself is a move in the right direction!) Never try to gain his comfort by criticizing him for not comforting you.[20]

Is the relationship of the criticizer to the "victim" significant to the amount of hurt caused by the criticism? What was Peter criticized for in Acts 11:1-3? How did it conclude in Acts 11:18? Was this the work of the Holy Spirit to create peace? Can the same peace happen today? How?

☆ Those Who Use Words Recklessly and Carelessly

According to Proverbs 12:18 do reckless words hurt? According to Jesus in Matthew 12:36-37, what is the consequence of speaking reckless words? Is it true that words can never hurt you? If you believe this in marriage, what happens? It is called divorce. Words can harden a heart and create divorce (Matt 19:8). What does Solomon call a "reckless worder" in Proverbs 14:16?

☆ People Who Speak Maliciously

Many verses in the Bible deal with malice: Exodus 23:1; Deuteronomy 19:16-17; Psalms 35:11; 41:5; 73:8; 139:20; Proverbs 26:24,26; Ezekiel 25:6; Daniel 3:8; Matthew 22:18; Acts 8:22; Romans 1:28f; 3 John 10. Realize that malice is condemned in the Scripture (1 Cor 5:8; Eph 4:31; Col 3:8; 1 Pet 2:1; Titus 3:3). The word "rid" means to "strip away; throw off." In 1 Corinthians 5:8 yeast is linked to malice. What two things should our new bread contain? How would these two traits improve communication?

1. According to Proverbs 26:24-26 what is the consequence of malice and deception? Malice means "nasty." How do these people get what they want? How do these people argue?
2. What does Solomon write about these people in Proverbs 22:8?
3. How did Paul describe malicious talkers in 1 Timothy 6:3-5? What words would you use to describe them?
4. According to Isaiah 58:9-10 what happens when people do away with malicious talking and finger pointing?
5. What five things did Peter tell people to get rid of in 1 Peter 2:1? How do you feel about getting rid of these things? Is the order of these things important? What would happen if you only got rid of some of them? Would they *grow* back even stronger if they were not totally eliminated? What does the word "all" mean? What is the opposite of the word "all"?

6. In Ephesians 4:31 what six things does Paul instruct people to get rid of?
7. In Colossians 3:8 what five things does Paul instruct people to get rid of? How does this idea of ridding ourselves of certain things relate to Deuteronomy 13:5; 17:7; 19:19; 21:21; 24:7 when it discusses purging evil from among Israel?

(Additional examples of malice: Esth 3:6; Ps 140:3; Prov 30:14; Isa 59:5; Matt 27:23; John 12:10; Acts 7:54.)

☆ **Mockers and Gloaters**
1. In Job 21:2-3 what did Job give his friends permission to do? Was he being sarcastic with his permission? Was Job's bad communication pattern of sarcasm done on purpose to make his friends think about what they were doing?
2. What did David not do when he was mocked according to Psalm 119:51?
3. What happens when you correct a mocker (Prov 9:7)? What consequence of being a mocker is found in Proverbs 9:12?
4. What happens to people who gloat over disasters according to Proverbs 17:5?
5. According to Proverbs 29:8, what does a mocker do? What do these people like to do after they win and you lose? Are these people good losers? Mockers have many characteristic statements such as, "He got what was coming to him," or, "I told you so." What does this type of communication create?

Solomon writes about mockers and gloaters in Proverbs 24:17-18: "Do not gloat when your enemy falls; when he stumbles, do not let your heart rejoice, or the LORD will see and disapprove and turn his wrath away from him."

☆ **Quarrelers**

1. According to Proverbs 15:18 what can a patient man do?
2. According to Proverbs 17:14 what should people do instead of quarreling?
3. What does a quarreler love according to Proverbs 17:19?
4. Who is quick to start a quarrel according to Proverbs 20:3? An honorable man does what?
5. According to Proverbs 21:19 it is better to live where than to live with a quarrelsome and ill-tempered wife?
6. To what does the writer of Proverbs 26:17 compare people who meddle in someone else's quarrel?
7. According to Proverbs 26:20 what feeds quarreling?
8. According to Proverbs 26:21 what do quarrels kindle?

When you quarrel with a fool, you might prove there are two. Who are some biblical characters who quarreled? Here is a short list:

> Abraham and Lot's herdsmen (Gen 13:6-18)
> Laban and Jacob (Gen 31:36-55)
> The Twelve Disciples (Mark 9:33-37; Luke 22:24-27)
> Christians in Jerusalem (Acts 15:1-35)
> Paul and Barnabas (Acts 15:36-41)
> Pharisees and Sadducees (Acts 23:6-10)

1. Did all of these quarrels have positive outcomes?
2. Why do many relationships become "the great debate"?
3. What were the relationships between those quarreling above?
4. According to 1 Timothy 3:2-7 what is the standard regarding quarreling to be for church leaders?
5. In 2 Timothy 2:14 what did Paul warn people about?

Causes of Quarreling

James 4:1-2, "What causes fights and quarrels among you? Don't they come from your desires that battle within you? You want something but don't get it. You kill and covet, but you cannot have what you want. You quarrel and fight. You do not have, because you do not ask God."

2 Timothy 2:23, "Don't have anything to do with foolish and stupid arguments, because you know they produce quarrels."

What makes it so hard for people to admit they are wrong? Is it because they would be admitting weakness, ignorance, or inappropriate self-esteem? What does Solomon write about these people in Proverbs 17:13-14? An evil man will pay evil for good and will always have evil around him. Starting a quarrel is like breaking a dam. So, drop it!

Biblical Solutions to Quarreling

Proverbs 15:1, "A gentle answer turns away wrath, but a harsh word stirs up anger."

Proverbs 15:8, "The LORD detests the sacrifice of the wicked, but the prayer of the upright pleases him."

Proverbs 25:15, "Through patience a ruler can be persuaded, and a gentle tongue can break a bone."

In Matthew 12:25-28 Jesus taught that unity calms a quarrel. Unity does not mean that there is constant agreement, but the same purpose, even though there is some disagreement. William Wrigley Jr., said, "When two men in business always agree, one of them is unnecessary."[21] Michel de Montaigne said, "There is no conversation more boring than the one where everybody agrees."[22] Dudley Field Malone said, "I have never in my life learned anything from any man who agreed with me."[23]

What did Paul say stops a quarrel? He said it was being compassionate, kind, humble, gentle, patient, and forgiving

(Col 3:12-13). He said it was being like-minded, having the same love, being one in spirit and purpose, not being selfish or conceited (Phil 2:1-2). Paul also taught that quarrels could be stopped by being kind, not resentful, and being gentle with instruction (2 Tim 2:24-25).

☆ **People Who Curse Bitterly**
   (Those Who Are Vulgar and Use Profanity)

The definitions of these words are nostalgic of an era of common decency. In the *New World Dictionary of American English* (third edition), it explains that "vulgar" comes from Latin meaning "the common people." *Vulgarity* is defined as "the state or quality of being vulgar, crude, coarse, unrefined." *Profane* is defined as "outside the temple, hence not sacred, showing disrespect or contempt for sacred things; irreverent." *Cursing* is defined as "to call evil or injury down, damn; obscene language; to swear or blaspheme."

Someone attempted to organize a step program like AA and NA. "Curse-a-holics Anonymous was an anti-profanity organization begun in Massachusetts to help people stop swearing. They even offered a 24-hour hot-line service. But they received so many foul-mouthed calls from irate swearers that they disbanded within a month."[24]

Scriptures Speak to the Foul-Tongued
   1. Exodus 20:7, "You shall not misuse the name of the LORD your God, for the LORD will not hold anyone guiltless who misuses his name."
   2. Psalm 10:7, "His mouth is full of curses and lies and threats; trouble and evil are under his tongue."
   3. Psalm 59:12, "For the sins of their mouths, for the words of their lips, let them be caught in their pride. For the curses and lies they utter, consume them in wrath . . . ."
   4. Psalm 109:17, "He loved to pronounce a curse—may

it come on him; he found no pleasure in blessing—
may it be far from him."

5. Ecclesiastes 7:22, "for you know in your heart that
   many times you yourself have cursed others."
6. Ephesians 4:31, "Get rid of all bitterness, rage and
   anger, brawling and slander, along with every form
   of malice."
7. James 3:9, "With the tongue we praise our Lord and
   Father, and with it we curse men, who have been
   made in God's likeness."

Points to Ponder

Has our society become desensitized to swearing? Is it
accepted as "normal"? What is the recent trend in the
media's use of profanity? Did Rhett Butler's parting shot at
Scarlett O'Hara in *Gone with the Wind* cause a problem
when it was first heard? Would it be offensive in today's
society? What does this reveal about our value disintegra-
tion?

Conclusion

Many of us were not raised to think, act, or talk like
Christians. We come from homes where gossip, slander, sarcasm, and swearing were the standard operating procedure
for everyone in our homes. When we become Christians, we
are to change these bad habits. It's easy to say, "But that's the
way I was raised. It's so ingrained, I can never change."
These thinking and speaking patterns were just as true for
the Greeks in Corinth or Athens or Philippi to whom Paul
preached. Yet Paul commanded that these habits be
dropped. How is it possible? Only through the power of the
Holy Spirit in our lives and a determination to be more
Christlike in our approach to others.

Thought for the Week

Life is short; make sure that your words bring enhancement and enjoyment to it.

Memory Verse for the Week

"Do not let any unwholesome talk come out of your mouths, but only what is helpful for building others up according to their needs, that it may benefit those who listen" (Eph 4:29).

Endnotes

1. LaHaye, *How to Be Happy*, p. 116.
2. Zodhiates, *Word Study Dictionary*, p. 1047.
3. Ibid., p. 340.
4. Ibid., p. 1477.
5. Ibid., p. 575.
6. Ibid., p. 999.
7. Ibid., p. 828.
8. Ibid., p. 1402.
9. Ibid., p. 149.
10. Ibid., p. 808.
11. Ibid., p. 100.
12. Ibid., p. 418.
13. Ibid., p. 1324.
14. Ibid., p. 850.
15. Associated Press (May 1990).
16. Condensed from "Toronto Fires Manager for Lies about Vietnam" (AP), *The StarPress*, Muncie, IN (March 18, 1999).
17. Terry Hekker, *Ever Since Adam and Eve* (New York: William Morrow and Co., 1979), p. 121.
18. Durham, *Speaking from the Heart*, p. 53.
19. Gary Smalley, *Hidden Keys of a Loving Lasting Marriage* (Grand Rapids: Zondervan, 1984), pp. 181-182.
20. Ibid., p. 276.
21. Parrott, *High-Maintenance*, p. 192.
22. Ibid., p. 193.
23. Ibid., p. 196.
24. Durham, *Speaking from the Heart*, p. 73.

Constructive
Communication

Chapter 8

Home on the Range

An Encouraging Word

An Encouraging Word

Home on the Range

Chapter 8

I like some of the old songs. I frequently listen to the "oldies" while I travel. The sad thing is that what are now considered oldies are the songs I grew up with. Now with contemporary artists performing remakes of old songs, my kids think they are listening to new songs. They are surprised to find that I know the words to these new songs before they do.

There is an old, old song we all know called "Home on the Range." The lyrics say, "Where seldom is heard a discouraging word, and the skies are not cloudy all day." It would be wonderful if this were the way real life was. In other words, edification only! The reality is that, where most of us live, seldom is heard an **encouraging** word.

If the quality of the heart is positive, then the by-product should be uplifting, encouraging words. If we could eliminate discouraging words, insults, and name calling, then disrespectful statements would also disappear. No belittling or berating! The world would become a much more positive place. Homes would be sweeter, work places would be a lot more tolerable and productive, and violence would decline.

This is not an unreachable utopian ideal. It is possible to communicate edification only. It takes a change of heart and a relationship with Jesus as Lord and Savior. It cannot be done by human effort only. People tend to get tired of being good after a little while.

How would this affect teammates if all they did was build up one another? What would happen if the coaches followed this same rule? Would players be willing to play harder for them? This type of encouragement would indeed be a rarity in today's sports. We learn from professional basketball:

> Losing already is taking its toll on the Detroit Pistons. Grant Hill — arguably the best player in the league — has been criticizing center Bison Dele (the former Brian Williams) for his lackadaisical play, asking Coach Alvin Gentry to bench him.
> Jerry Stackhouse has been calling Hill a ballhog. Hill thinks that Stackhouse is nuts. And Dele seems oblivious to it all.[1]

This type of criticism might have been used to try to motivate the players to play harder. Usually, however, this type of motivation only creates hard feelings and destroys unity. Criticism greatly affects teamwork and chemistry. The damage caused by these words may be irreparable.

Edification Only

Edification is a great word. In Greek it is *oikodome*, meaning "the act of building."[2] One of the derivatives of this word is frequently used as a construction term: edifice (building). Edification as a speech term means to build up, strengthen, and uplift. This pattern, if practiced, would be an excellent witness for Christ to a negative, sarcastic world. People would see and hear his life and light shining through this speech pattern (Matt 5:15-16).

Edification is the only prescribed form of communication mentioned in Scripture. The biblical fact is that edification in communication is God's will! Edification should occur at all times. Paul wrote, "Do not let any unwholesome talk come out of your mouths, but only what is helpful for building others up according to their needs, that it may benefit those who listen" (Eph 4:29).

When is edification needed the most? When a person is hurting, tired, frustrated, lonely, scared, unemployed, mad, and disappointed. The truth is it is needed at all times and in a variety of ways.

Seeking the Positive

I guess Grandma was right when she said, "If you can't think of something good to say, don't say anything at all." Why is this advice so hard to follow? It goes against our human nature. If we can't think of something positive to say about another person, the problem lies with the speaker!

What are some remedies for not being able to think of positives in people? Jesus made his disciples spend two days in Samaria eating and living with Samaritans (John 4). When the disciples did this, surely it improved the way they saw the Samaritans. It would also have improved the way the Samaritans saw the Jews. I am sure this was Jesus' goal. He used this "field trip" to break down prejudice between two groups of people. How many groups can you think of today that would benefit from this kind of field trip?

If "edification only" was the rule in our homes, divorce and family breakups would not be as prevalent. We would avoid a tremendous amount of stress and dissension. Edification only would create a peace that would be unshakable (Isa 54:10). Every relationship in the home would greatly improve. It would enhance self-esteem. It is too bad that this is not an easy change. We seem resistant to positive communication changes.

Which are more readily accepted, compliments or criticisms? As surprising as it may seem, criticism often feels more comfortable than compliments because of our negative communication habits. Compliments are very hard to give and receive. It is often easier for us to write a compliment than give one verbally. We need to learn to be better at giving and receiving compliments. This learning takes place best with practice, practice, practice.

Edification as Part of Communication

According to Ephesians 4:29, communication must meet needs. It should meet physical, emotional, spiritual, social, and intellectual needs. Communication must benefit those who listen. Edification easily accomplishes these goals. Edification empowers people during times of failure and frustration. It helps people focus on their positive attributes instead of dwelling on the negative ones.

Paul's writings contain several passages that deal with communication. I want to highlight several of them that deal with *edification*. These may actually be the toughest verses on communication in the Bible because they go completely against our human nature. Humans tend to be negative by nature and positive only by learning and the influence of others.

Paul wrote about edification: "Let us therefore make every effort to do what leads to peace and to mutual edification" (Rom 14:19). Every effort means *every* effort! Edification will usually require much work but will lead to peaceful relationships. "Mutual" means that both the listener and the speaker benefit when edifying speech is used.

"Each of us should please his neighbor for his good, to build him up" (Rom 15:2). According to Jesus (Luke 10:25-37) our neighbor is anyone we meet, even strangers along the road. We all know lots of neighbors who would greatly benefit from our edifying lips. "For even if I boast somewhat freely about the authority the Lord gave us for building you up rather than pulling you down, I will not be ashamed of it" (2 Cor 10:8). Christians have the same authority today. It is not implemented as often as God would like. We need to edify everyone we encounter.

"This is why I write these things when I am absent, that when I come I may not have to be harsh in my use of authority—the authority the Lord gave me for building you up, not for tearing you down" (2 Cor 13:10). I can think of no time in Scripture where Jesus put people down or made fun of anyone. He could have done it with Zacchaeus who was a hated tax collector (Luke 19:1-10). Jesus could have let this vulnerable little person really have it. Instead Jesus shared a meal with him. It changed Zacchaeus forever.

"Therefore encourage one another and build each other up, just as in fact you are doing" (1 Thess 5:11). If the church was already doing this, why would Paul write this? It was a gentle reminder to help them continue to edify one another. It seems that this idea of encouragement can be easily forgotten.

Barnabas—A Lifelong Encourager

Can you think of any good encouragers mentioned in the Bible? If you were to read through the Book of Acts, you would soon run across a man named Barnabas. "Joseph, a Levite from Cyprus, whom the apostles called Barnabas (which means Son of Encouragement), sold a field he owned and brought the money and put it at the apostles' feet" (Acts 4:36-37). Throughout the book of Acts, we see many deeds performed by Barnabas which encouraged and edified the church. In Acts 9, we see Barnabas willingly embracing the newly converted Saul. Barnabas testifies of the genuine conversion of Paul, convincing the Jerusalem congregation of Saul's devotion to his new life. We see evidence of Barnabas's encouraging spirit again in Acts 11. Here Barnabas is able to edify the members of the Antioch church. "When he [Barnabas] arrived and saw the evidence of the grace of God, he was glad and encouraged them all to remain true to the Lord with all their hearts. He was a good man, full of the Holy Spirit and faith, and a great number of people were brought to the Lord" (Acts 11:23-24).

These three examples alone show Barnabas's encouraging nature. He saw the best in a person. He was slow to criticize and quick to forgive. Barnabas regularly practiced edification, and the church body benefited because of it.

Building Up versus Tearing Down

Affirmation is synonymous with edification. Wayne T. and Nancy Alderson say of affirmation, "When affirmation abounds and creates trust, communication begins to flow." They also write, "The more we communicate with people who affirm us and whom we trust, the more we are loyal to the people."[3]

If we can build people up, we can also tear them down. When you tear others down, why do they frequently return the favor and tear you down? Is this fulfilling the golden rule in reverse? "So in everything, do to others what you would have them do to you, for this sums up the Law and the Prophets" (Matt 7:12). This rule of Jesus was not intended to work this way. Encouraging words fulfill this law. The New Testament gives us many examples of this rule put into practice.

Romans 12:6-8 reminds us that encouragement is a gift given by God: ". . . if it is encouraging, let him encourage; if it is contributing to the needs of others, let him give generously; if it is leadership, let him govern diligently; if it is showing mercy, let him do it cheerfully." We are the only creation of God's that can edify. God did this by design. We must use this gift as God intended.

"I am sending him to you for this very purpose, that you may know how we are, and that he may *encourage* you" (Eph 6:22).

"I am sending him to you for the express purpose that you may know about our circumstances and that he may *encourage* your hearts" (Col 4:8).

"We sent Timothy, who is our brother and God's fellow worker in spreading the gospel of Christ, to strengthen and *encourage* you in your faith . . ." (1 Thess 3:2).

"Therefore *encourage* each other with these words" (1 Thess 4:18).

"And we urge you, brothers, warn those who are idle, *encourage* the timid, help the weak, be patient with everyone" (1 Thess 5:14).

"Preach the Word; be prepared in season and out of season; correct, rebuke and *encourage*—with great patience and careful instruction" (2 Tim 4:2).

"He must hold firmly to the trustworthy message as it has been taught, so that he can *encourage* others by sound doctrine and refute those who oppose it" (Titus 1:9). Encouragement from unsound doctrine produces false hope.

"These, then, are the things you should teach. *Encourage* and rebuke with all authority. Do not let anyone despise you" (Titus 2:15). It is strange that encouragement and rebuking can be in the same sentence, but the root of both of these is love.

"But *encourage* one another daily, as long as it is called Today, so that none of you may be hardened by sin's deceitfulness" (Heb 3:13).

"Let us not give up meeting together, as some are in the habit of doing, but let us *encourage* one another—and all the more as you see the Day approaching" (Heb 10:25). Daily encouragement is necessary and needed in a depressing, sad, joy-killing world.

Conclusion

In closing this chapter on edification and encouragement, I want to encourage you to become more like Jesus. He was practiced in encouragement, affirmation, and edification. Put this principle of encouragement into practice. Encourage everyone you see. Not with shallow remarks, but with words that are sincere, meaningful, and important. It is my hope and prayer that this chapter made you more aware of how you should communicate. Improvements can always be made. The children of the King need to speak the language of royalty and love in a fallen world. What a tremendous witness!

Thought for the Week

Those who are edifiers are frequently the ones who need to be edified. They edify others, but they may have no one to edify them.

Memory Verses for the Week

"Let us therefore make every effort to do what leads to peace and mutual edification" (Rom 14:19).

"Do not rebuke an older man harshly, but exhort him as if he were your father. Treat younger men as brothers, older women as mothers, and younger women as sisters, with absolute purity" (1 Tim 5:1-2).

Endnotes

1. "Pistons Turning on Each Other as Losses Mount," *The Orlando Sentinel*, as quoted in *The Star Press*, Muncie, IN, (February 22, 1999).

2. W. E. Vine, Merrill F. Unger, and William White, Jr., *Vine's Complete Expository Dictionary of Old and New Testament Words* (Nashville: Thomas Nelson, 1985), p. 194.

3. Wayne T. Alderson and Nancy Alderson, *Theory R Management* (Nashville: Thomas Nelson, 1994), p. 62.

Chapter 9

Bite Your Tongue

Restraining the Tongue

Restraining the Tongue

Bite Your Tongue

Chapter 9

My dad was an avid golfer. He loved to play the game but also enjoyed watching it on TV. One of the "rules" of the house when golf was on the tube was that we had to be quiet if we were going to watch with him. This chapter is not on being quiet during golf, but on restraining the tongue, or not speaking at certain times when it is deemed best to be silent and still. Proverbs 15:28 teaches restraint of the tongue, "The heart of the righteous weighs its answers . . . ." This is what it means to *restrain* the tongue, to weigh an answer before speaking.

I recently heard an interesting quote about the tongue on a Christian radio station, "It weighs almost nothing, but few can hold it!" Why is the tongue so difficult to hold? One of the reasons could be because the option of speaking is more desirable than not speaking. Ogden Nash said to a group of men (but it also applies to women), "To keep your marriage brimming with love in the loving cup, when you're wrong admit it, when you're right shut up."[1]

A young English professor at a local university was stopped for speeding as he was late for class. The policeman gave him a warning ticket and told him, "Drive safe." The professor wanted to show his intelligence, so he corrected the policeman's grammar by saying, "It is *safely*—you said safe." At this the policeman went back to the patrol car and wrote out a $75.00 ticket and gave it to the professor. Had he kept his mouth shut, it would have saved him money—and he would have seemed more intelligent.

The Facts about Silence

People tend to interpret silence incorrectly. Consider a first date, where there is a thirty-second lull in conversation. The couple begins to think the date is taking a disastrous turn. The man may think, "She doesn't like me," while the girl may think, "I must be making a terrible impression." Both of these interpretations could be dangerous for the future of that relationship. This silence can create panic!

I know a lot of people who are "afraid" of silence. They interpret it as a sign that something is wrong. However, remember the saying "silence is golden." Silence does not necessarily indicate that something is wrong. On the contrary, it could indicate that we are doing the right thing. We simply need to learn to interpret silence correctly. "In human intercourse the tragedy begins. Not where there is misunderstanding about words, but when silence is not understood— Thoreau, *A Week on the Concord and Merrimack Rivers.*"[2]

In his book *Spiritual Disciplines for the Christian Life,* Donald S. Whitney lists the practice of silence and solitude as a discipline of the Christian life. He defines the discipline of silence as "the voluntary and temporary abstention from speaking so that certain spiritual goals might be sought."[3] It is possible to learn to utilize silence correctly. Understanding this discipline will not only enhance our spiritual life but will also help benefit our earthly relationships.

If we are to learn the value of silence, we must know when it is most appropriate to use it. We should not speak hastily when we or the people with whom we are speaking are

→ hurting
→ angry or frustrated
→ afraid
→ tired
→ hungry
→ rushed or hurried
→ sick.

We are often at our most vulnerable at these times. If we were to speak to someone who was experiencing one of these conditions or if we ourselves are, we open the door to potential harmful communication. The control of the tongue is often weakened during these times. With defenses weakened or defeated, words can come out like ash and lava from volcanoes. They can harm in a matter of seconds. It is better to walk away and wait for a more appropriate time to talk. Remember, what you say can never be taken back. Practicing silence may just save a relationship.

Old Testament Teachings on the Value of Silence

Joseph should have learned to keep his mouth shut. It was bad enough that his father loved him more than the other brothers (Gen 37:4). It was bad enough that Joseph was a snitch and told his father about what his brothers were doing or not doing (Gen 37:2). It was bad enough that his father showed favoritism to Joseph by giving him the coat of many colors (Gen 37:3). But Joseph had to tell his brothers about two dreams he had: One was about their sheaves of grain bowing down to his sheaf (Gen 37:6-7), and the second dream consisted of the sun, moon, and eleven stars bowing down to him (Gen 37:9). Joseph probably learned the value

of restraint when his brothers, who were fed up with his atti-
tude, sold him into slavery.

Often in the Old Testament, God's people were commanded to be still and quiet when in his presence in worship. The same principle can apply to us today when we
worship God. There are benefits to remaining silent during
worship. We are commanded to be silent in the holy temple
of God (Hab 2:20). We are commanded to be silent before the
presence of the LORD (Zeph 1:7; Zech 2:13). David wrote, "Be
still, and know that I am God; I will be exalted among the
nations, I will be exalted in the earth" (Ps 46:10).

Solomon wrote, "A man of knowledge uses words with
restraint, and a man of understanding is even-tempered"
(Prov 17:27). He is not writing here about withholding certain emotions when they are appropriate. It is not wrong to
express emotions. We do need to be careful of the manner in
which we express those emotions. When we allow our
mouth to speak without restraint, we often say things we
should have left unsaid.

We know from Scripture that silence can be beneficial
when one wishes to comfort a grieving person. Sometimes
words only intensify grief, whereas the simple, quiet presence of a good friend can actually help the grieving person.
Elisha commanded the prophets of Bethel to be quiet about
Elijah being taken by the Lord (2 Kgs 2:1-5). He did not wish
to speak of the impending loss of his mentor and teacher. He
knew that words would not help ease the loss. Job told his
"friends" to be silent because their talking amounted to fool-
ishness (Job 13:5). Their so-called advice and counsel wounded
Job more than the tragedies he suffered.

Jesus and Silence

This is more of a side note to the subject of speech, but
not using words can speak volumes. As the Creator of

speech, Jesus knew when and how to use words. The reasons for silence are as varied as the times Jesus was silent or commanded silence.

Jesus chose silence at certain encounters. He was silent with the woman who had a demon-possessed daughter (Matt 15:21-23). Here we find a typical male response to tears: "Send her away," the disciples urged Jesus, "for she keeps crying out after us." (Matt 15:23). Was Jesus testing the disciples' response to her tears? Perhaps Jesus would have liked the disciples to be more compassionate to her hurting and tears. Their response could be seen as apathetic. How do *you* respond to the tears of a stranger? How about the tears of a close companion? Can you more easily empathize with one? Or are both awkward for you?

Jesus was silent when he was questioned by the accusers of the woman caught in adultery (John 8:3-6). When he spoke, he spoke words that forever rang in their ears, "If any one of you is without sin, let him be the first to throw a stone at her" (v. 7). The result of these nineteen words was that they saved a life and made a lifetime impact.

Jesus commanded people to be silent. He commanded the man he healed of leprosy to be silent (Matt 8:1-4). At the healing of the two blind men he commanded them to keep silent (9:27-30), but they did not do what he asked (Matt 9:31). He warned the people he healed not to tell others who he was (Matt 12:15-16). After Peter's confession, he warned the disciples to tell no one he was the Christ (Matt 16:13-20; Mark 8:27-30). After the transfiguration, Jesus told Peter, James, and John to tell no one what they saw until he was raised from the dead (Matt 17:1-9). He commanded evil spirits not to tell who he was (Mark 3:10-12). He gave strict orders to Peter, James, John, and the parents not to say anything about raising a girl from the dead (Mark 5:37-43). He commanded a leper to be quiet about his healing (Luke 5:14).

Some have intimidated others with silence. People rebuked blind Bartimaeus to keep quiet when he sought

Jesus' healing (Mark 10:46-48). He did not listen, and he kept saying, "Son of David, have mercy on me!" Because of his persistence Jesus heard his plea and healed him (Mark 10:48-52).

Jesus chose silence in the midst of trials. Jesus was silent before the High Priest (Matt 26:57-63). He was silent before Pilate (Matt. 27:12-14). He was silent before Herod (Luke 23:8-12). Jesus was silent in these situations because he knew his words would not be received as intended. "Therefore the prudent man keeps quiet in such times, for the times are evil" (Amos 5:13).

Conclusion

Taming the tongue is humanly impossible according to James 3:8. Restraining the tongue may be the closest we ever get to taming it. We need to learn when to be silent. Silence may indeed be golden if it is well timed in our dealings with others. We can imitate the examples from James, Paul, and Jesus. We can learn the effectiveness of a well-bitten tongue.

Thought for the Week

Frank Outlaw admonished, "Watch your thoughts; they become words. Watch your words; they become actions. Watch your actions; they become habits. Watch your habits; they become character. Watch your character; it becomes your destiny."

Memory Verses for the Week

"He who answers before listening—that is his folly and shame" (Prov 18:13).

"Whoever would love life and see good days must keep his tongue from evil and his lips from deceitful speech" (1 Pet 3:10).

"He who guards his lips guards his life, but he who speaks rashly will come to ruin" (Prov 13:3).

Endnotes

1. H. Norman Wright, *Communication: Key to Your Marriage* (Ventura, CA: Regal Books, 1980), p. 157.

2. Cited in Charles R. Swindoll, *The Mystery of God's Will: What Does He Want for Me?* (Nashville, TN: Word, 1999), p. 96.

3. Donald S. Whitney, *Spiritual Disciplines for the Christian Life* (Colorado Springs: Navpress, 1991), p. 176.

Chapter 10

Improving Listening and Communication

Improving Listening and Communication
Chapter 10

Every person has a deep desire and need to be heard and understood. *Listening* is more than hearing words. It involves having insight, wisdom, and discernment with what is being said as well as what is not being said.

Ken Durham offers several suggestions to getting beyond small talk and becoming a better listener:

➠ Encourage others to talk about their interests, opinions, and feelings.
➠ Learn people's names when you first meet them.
➠ Don't attack defensiveness when you encounter it.
➠ Create opportunities for unpressured communication in a comfortable setting.
➠ Always keep a confidence.
➠ Don't be argumentative.
➠ You cannot force self-disclosure on others.
➠ Admit to others your faults, needs, and fears.[1]

Dr. C. Everett Koop published an article about listening entitled "Trailblazers of the Century," in which he compares modern medical practices with those of yesteryear:

Years ago, doctors listened more. We didn't have the myriad tests we have now. The art of diagnosis was to listen to the patient's history and put it together as a detective would. A recent study found that when patients come to a doctor with a complaint, male physicians interrupt them within 17 seconds, female physicians within 45 seconds. Only 1 in 52 patients leave that kind of encounter feeling, "I told my story and the doctor listened to me." Managed care has made the relationship no better, because companies limit the time doctors can spend with patients.[2]

Biblical Teachings on Listening

Is it true that to understand you first have to listen? The Bible teaches this concept. Throughout the Old and New Testament, we see that wisdom and understanding only come with listening. We see from the life of Christ that he was the model listener and set the perfect example for us in this area.

Eccelesiates 5:1 speaks about listening, "Guard your steps when you go to the house of God. Go near to listen rather than to offer the sacrifice of fools, who do not know that they do wrong." Solomon teaches what can be gained from listening: "let the wise listen and add to their learning, and let the discerning get guidance" (Prov 1:5). Solomon wrote that listeners "will be at home among the wise" (Prov 15:31). Listening will cause a person to stay on the right path and be wise (Prov 23:19). Solomon wrote that people should listen to their fathers and not despise their mothers (Prov 23:22).

Wisdom has an incredible effect on both parts of communication, speaking and listening. Solomon wrote that we should,

> . . . accept my words and store up my commands within you, turning your ear to wisdom and applying your heart to understanding, and if you call out for insight and cry aloud

for understanding, and if you look for it as for silver and search for it as for hidden treasure, then you will understand the fear of the LORD and find the knowledge of God (Prov 2:1-5).

Solomon added,

Then you will understand what is right and just and fair—every good path. For wisdom will enter your heart, and knowledge will be pleasant to your soul. Discretion will protect you, and understanding will guard you. Wisdom will save you from the ways of wicked men, from men whose words are perverse (Prov 2:9-12).

Jesus was a good listener. He listened to people talk about things he already knew. In Mark 6:30-31, it says about Jesus, "The apostles gathered around Jesus and reported to him all they had done and taught. Then, because so many people were coming and going that they did not even have a chance to eat, he said to them, 'Come with me by yourselves to a quiet place and get some rest.'" In Luke 10:17 it says, "The seventy-two returned with joy and said, 'Lord, even the demons submit to us in your name.'"

Jesus allowed them to talk about what they did because he knew it was very important for them to express their excitement. Their talking and his listening was also a way of getting rid of a lot of emotional energy. Look at Jesus' response to them in Luke 10:21, "At that time Jesus, full of joy through the Holy Spirit, said, 'I praise you, Father, Lord of heaven and earth, because you have hidden these things from the wise and learned, and revealed them to little children. Yes, Father, for this was your good pleasure.'" Listening brought great joy to Jesus, and it can to us as well. We should look on the opportunity to listen to the stories of others as a great blessing.

Improving Listening

Here are six simple things you can do to improve your listening skills.

- ☛ *Listening shows love.* To let people know that you love them, you must listen to what they are saying and be genuinely interested.
- ☛ *Look at who is talking to you.*
- ☛ *Stop whatever you are doing when you're being spoken to.* Minimize distractions. Turn off the TV or stereo if needed. It is hard to listen to two things at once. You will usually pay attention to one more than the other. Give the person who is speaking your full attention—no matter how young she is or what she is talking about. This is a great way to build her esteem and improve relationships.
- ☛ *Get up and go to the same room as the person you are talking to.* Don't ask him to come to you. Walls are barriers to effective communication. Any comment that is yelled will be seen as a negative statement.
- ☛ *Maintain concentration on the topic* by focusing on what is being said and not on what you're going to say after the other person has finished talking.
- ☛ *Ask questions to clarify conversation.* Asking questions at appropriate times will not only improve your understanding of the topic, but will also show that you are genuinely listening.

Tim LaHaye suggests six excellent ways to improve communication.

- ➢ Pray for the wisdom of God and the filling of the Holy Spirit.
- ➢ Plan a time that is good for your partner.
- ➢ Speak the truth in love.
- ➢ Don't lose your temper.
- ➢ Allow for reaction time.
- ➢ Commit the problem to God.[3]

Several Ways to Stop Communication

If there are good listening skills, there are also some bad ones. Four bad listening skills (some of which were touched on in what *to* do) are:

☎ Split attention: listening while you are doing something else.

☎ Hurry up behaviors: tapping your fingers; formulating your response before the person is finished speaking; rolling the hand and arm telling the person to hurry up.

☎ Sentence completion: filling in words before the person is through talking.

☎ Defensiveness of comment: automatic defensiveness about what is being said. Taking things immediately negatively.

Some behaviors which will stop communication cold are

◊ Temper tantrums
◊ Stamping
◊ Screaming
◊ Throwing things
◊ Bringing up past negative events of the other person
◊ Spitting at or near the other person.

These may sound funny, but we all know people who have used the above methods. There are learned behaviors that are highly effective at breaking down communication. Gary Smalley has compiled a list similar to the one at the beginning of this section expressing several ways people "show" they are not listening to the person's advice. Some of them are

✌ picking up the newspaper or sewing while the other person is talking
✌ rolling your eyes
✌ yawning
✌ criticizing before you've heard your partner out
✌ trying to get in the last word[4]

All of the above will only harm communication. We must break these bad habits if we wish to improve our communication skills.

Four Fighting Patterns or "Friday Night at the Fights"

Any time we are close to someone and spend a lot of time with that person, there are likely to be occasional fights. *How* we fight is critical to maintaining a healthy relationship. As you read these descriptions of various types of fighting patterns, note how listening as well as speaking and acting are involved in each one.

1. "Gravity fights": No matter what topic the fight begins on, it goes down to one central issue that has not been resolved yet. The only outcome of this fight is hurt and harm. Nothing gets accomplished but hurt feelings. This type of fighting is cyclical in nature. The issue that is brought up is usually the result of bitterness and unforgiveness. There are several "good" gravity issues that can do a tremendous amount of damage to an already wounded heart and relationship. Three of these topics are: a past abortion, an adulterous relationship, or irresponsibility of how money was spent years ago. These types of issues cause rifts in relationships and marriages unless they are resolved.

2. "Smorgasbord fights": A lot of different issues are brought up during the same fight. Nothing usually gets resolved in this type of fighting because it is overwhelming to deal with so many different topics.

3. "'Thar she blows' fights": This is when a person has taken a lot of negative stuff in and internalized it. The person will eventually explode when the pressure becomes too great. This particular fighting pattern is nasty because it can involve months' or even years' worth of anger and bitterness.

4. "Issue fights": A topic of importance and significance is brought up and it is dealt with in an appropriate time and method. Healing can occur with this type of argument.

If we do have to bring up a topic which we know will create an argument, Chuck Swindoll gives several rules on how to fight fairly.

> be honest and respectful
> keep it under control
> keep it timed right
> keep it positive
> keep it tactful
> keep it private
> keep it cleaned up (forgive, be kind and tender after the fighting is done)[5]

Gregory J.P. Godek discusses guidelines for what he calls "Courtship Conversation."

✓ Talk to one another with respect.
✓ Remember that conversation involves two-way communication.
✓ No judging, assuming, or second-guessing the other person.
✓ Complete honesty is demanded, assumed, and never questioned.
✓ Speak from the heart, but don't leave the head behind.
✓ Maintain eye contact.
✓ Practice with each other at least one hour a day.[6]

Conclusion

We have heard that to be a good counselor, we must be a good listener. Common sense tells us that God created us with two ears and one mouth in order to listen twice as much as we talk. Listening is as much (or more) a part of communication as talking!

Thought for the Week

Disagreements are not personal attacks. They are natural and normal. Don't overreact to them. Be patient and gentle with your words and behavior in times of conflict.

Memory Verses for the Week

"Do everything without complaining or arguing . . ." (Phil 2:14).

"The Sovereign LORD has given me an instructed tongue, to know the word that sustains the weary. He wakens me morning by morning, wakens my ear to listen like one being taught" (Isa 50:4).

Endnotes

1 Durham, *Speaking from the Heart*, p. 94.

2 *Publishers Weekly* (March 29, 1999).

3 LaHaye, *How to Be Happy*, pp. 121-122.

4 Smalley, *HiddenKeys*, p. 268.

5 Condensed from Charles R. Swindoll, *Strike the Original Match: Rekindling and Preserving Your Marriage Fire* (Portland, OR: Multnomah, 1980), pp. 103-111.

6 Gregory J.P. Godek, *1001 Ways to Be Romantic* (Boston: Casablanca Press, 1995), p. 167.

God's Word
on the
Subject

Chapter 11

Solomon's Wisdom on Communication

Solomon's Wisdom on Communication

Chapter 11

Proverbs is one of my favorite books in the Bible. I refer to it many times a day in my counseling practice. One of the most common topics found in the book of Proverbs is communication. The book is loaded with speech advice! Solomon must have understood the importance of being able to speak well. He had to because of his occupation as king and because of all his wives!

Though we have briefly discussed the virtues of the Proverbs earlier in this book, let's take a more in-depth look at several of the verses Solomon wrote.

Proverbs 4:24 — "Put away perversity from your mouth; keep corrupt talk far from your lips." If a person is going to keep perversity away from his mouth, he has to keep it away from his heart and mind.

Proverbs 6:2 — ". . . if you have been trapped by what you said, ensnared by the words of your mouth . . ." Words can easily be a trap and a snare. Words can trap people into doing things they really don't want to do.

Proverbs 6:19 — ". . . a false witness who pours out lies and a man who stirs up dissension among brothers." The tongue can be filled with lies and stir up trouble. On the other side of the Word Paul wrote to Titus on this topic, "But avoid foolish controversies and genealogies and arguments and quarrels about the law, because these are unprofitable and useless. Warn a divisive person once, and then warn him a second time. After that, have nothing to do with him" (Titus 3:9-10).

Solomon wrote about things that God detests and hates, "There are six things the LORD hates, seven that are detestable to him: haughty eyes, a lying tongue, hands that shed innocent blood, a heart that devises wicked schemes, feet that are quick to rush into evil, a false witness who pours out lies and a man who stirs up dissension among brothers (Prov 6:16-19). Herman Bezzel writes, "White lies are silken threads that bind us to the Enemy, invisible webs that are woven in hell."[1] Lies are one of the enemy's greatest weapons (John 8:44).

Proverbs 8:13 — "To fear the LORD is to hate evil; I hate pride and arrogance, evil behavior and perverse speech." The word "perverse" used here means "to turn about or over; to change, overturn or pervert."[2] Paul wrote about people not becoming arrogant (Rom 11:20). Pride and arrogance create terrible communication patterns. It is the proud and arrogant who put others down. They are the ones who can easily create arguments and fights.

Proverbs 10:18-21 — "He who conceals his hatred has lying lips, and whoever spreads slander is a fool. When words are many, sin is not absent, but he who holds his tongue is wise. The tongue of the righteous is choice silver, but the heart of the wicked is of little value. The lips of the righteous nourish many, but fools die for lack of judgment." One of the reasons many words are considered sinful is because it takes many words for rationalizing and making excuses.

Proverbs 12:13-14 — "An evil man is trapped by his sinful talk, but a righteous man escapes trouble. From the fruit of his lips a man is filled with good things as surely as the work of his hands rewards him." All words produce something (Proverbs 13:2). Some words produce love and peace, while other words can produce hatred and strife.

Proverbs 12:22 — "The LORD detests lying lips, but he delights in men who are truthful." God delights in truthful words because this is who he is (John 14:6). We are told to imitate God (Eph 5:1).

Proverbs 14:3 — "A fool's talk brings a rod to his back, but the lips of the wise protect them." Words can protect or bring a beating.

Proverbs 15:1 — "A gentle answer turns away wrath, but a harsh word stirs up anger." This is mirror communication, the way you treat others is the way they will treat you. If you are hateful, the hearer can also produce hatred. Being gentle to others typically makes them gentle with you. Remember the old saying, "You can get a horse to mind better with sugar than with a whip." This means that we should not communicate when we are angry. (For further reference about this topic see: Prov 25:15; 29:11; Eph 4:26-27,31).

What did Nehemiah do when he was angry about the way his countrymen were being treated? (Nehemiah 5:6-8). He pondered what he wanted to do with his anger. Then he spoke to the people with whom he was angry. He spoke with words they could not defeat, so they remained quiet (v. 8). This is a great way of dealing with anger in communication.

Proverbs 15:23 — "A man finds joy in giving an apt reply —

and how good is a timely word!" Words can be timely and appropriate. They can also be untimely and inappropriate.

Proverbs 16:13 — "Kings take pleasure in honest lips; they value a man who speaks the truth."

Proverbs 16:24 — "Pleasant words are a honeycomb, sweet to the soul and healing to the bones." Pleasant words are like candy. They can also be attractive and desirable to others.

Proverbs 18:2 — "A fool finds no pleasure in understanding but delights in airing his own opinions." A fool enjoys hearing *himself* talk. It is also hard for him to listen to others.

Proverbs 18:4 — "The words of a man's mouth are deep waters, but the fountain of wisdom is a bubbling brook." Words show the deepness of a person's character and commitments. People can also be shallow.

Proverbs 18:13 — "He who answers before listening — that is his folly and his shame." This verse describes partial listening which can be dangerous. It is probably written more to men and dads who may be more prone than women to hear only half of what their wife or children say before jumping in with a response. A person who does not listen will be seen as foolish and shameful. In Job 21:2 Job advises, "Listen carefully to my words; let this be the consolation you give me." In Job 21:3 he told his friends, "Bear with me while I speak, and after I have spoken, mock on." What did he tell his friends they could do after they listened to him? If they insisted on mocking Job, they could listen for justification of their commentary.

Proverbs 18:20-21 — "From the fruit of his mouth a man's stomach is filled; with the harvest from his lips he is satisfied. The tongue has the power of life and death, and those who love it will eat its fruit." The tongue has power — power to heal and power to destroy. Hebrews 13:15 says, "Through Jesus, therefore, let us continually offer to God a sacrifice of praise—the fruit of lips that confess his name." This is a truly powerful use of the tongue.

Proverbs 20:25—"It is a trap for a man to dedicate something rashly and only later to consider his vows." Words can be like a Chinese finger puzzle. The more you try to get out of them, the more they entrap you.

Proverbs 21:6—"A fortune made by a lying tongue is a fleeting vapor and a deadly snare." Lying lips often create fleeting relationships as well.

Proverbs 22:11—"He who loves a pure heart and whose speech is gracious will have the king for his friend." This person distinguishes himself by his lips. He will make a name for himself by his speech and heart.

Proverbs 23:9—"Do not speak to a fool, for he will scorn the wisdom of your words." Fools do not listen to words spoken by the wise and righteous. You are wasting your breath.

Proverbs 25:11—"A word aptly spoken is like apples of gold in settings of silver." Words can be appropriate and like fine jewelry. They can also be cheap imitations, like costume jewelry.

Proverbs 25:15—"Through patience a ruler can be persuaded, and a gentle tongue can break a bone." Patience is described as being persuasive, and gentleness is described as being powerful. Patience and gentleness have the Holy Spirit in common (see Gal 5:22-23). Jesus' brother James wrote, "But the wisdom that comes from heaven is first of all pure; then peace-loving, considerate, submissive, full of mercy and good fruit, impartial and sincere" (Jas 3:17). Wisdom is a main ingredient in effective, accurate communication.

Proverbs 26:4-5—"Do not answer a fool according to his folly, or you will be like him yourself. Answer a fool according to his folly, or he will be wise in his own eyes." Answering a fool proves there are at least two in the world. If we get down to his communication level, he wins!

Proverbs 26:18-20 — "Like a madman shooting firebrands or deadly arrows is a man who deceives his neighbor and says, 'I was only joking!' Without wood a fire goes out; without gossip a quarrel dies down." The word "deceive" is a gentle word for lies. The power of gossip is found in starting quarrels.

Proverbs 26:24-25 — "A malicious man disguises himself with his lips, but in his heart he harbors deceit. Though his speech is charming, do not believe him, for seven abominations fill his heart." The word "harbor" means "to dock or hold." A disguise is a costume or a mask that is used to hide.

Proverbs 26:28 — "A lying tongue hates those it hurts, and a flattering mouth works ruin." Lies hurt respect and trust. Flattery does the same thing when it is found out to be false or said with hidden motives. François de la Rochefoucauld said, "Flattery is a kind of bad money, to which our vanity gives us currency."[3]

Proverbs 27:14 — "If a man loudly blesses his neighbor early in the morning, it will be taken as a curse." No one likes to be woken up too early, even to be blessed. Loud, early communication is likely to be interpreted as a curse.

Proverbs 29:20 — "Do you see a man who speaks in haste? There is more hope for a fool than for him." Speaking in haste means to speak quickly, usually without much thought to what is being said. One possible reason there is more hope for a fool than a person who speaks in haste is because people may feel sorry for the fool and give him a second chance. People may not be as gracious with a person who speaks in haste.

Proverbs 31:26 — "She speaks with wisdom, and faithful instruction is on her tongue." Once again there is a link between wisdom and proper communication. This time the link is also between wisdom and godliness. This trait is hard to find in today's society.

Thought for the Week

The words "always" and "never" can be lies. When you say these words you may be misspeaking. Be careful with overgeneralizing comments.

Memory Verse for the Week

"The quiet words of the wise are more to be heeded than the shouts of a ruler of fools" (Eccl 9:17).

Endnotes

1. Cited in Durham, *Speaking from the Heart*, p. 42.

2. Spiros Zodhiates, ed., "Hebrew and Chaldee Dictionary," *The Hebrew-Greek Key Study Bible* (Chattanooga, TN: AMG, 1990), p. 33.

3. Cited in Parrott, *High -Maintenance*, p. 181.

Chapter 12

James and Paul on Communication

James and Paul on Communication

Chapter 12

Practical Advice for Communication from James

James is a book full of practical advice. It is the Proverbs of the New Testament. Like Proverbs, James devotes a lot of time to discussing communication. He wrote, "My dear brothers, take note of this: Everyone should be quick to listen, slow to speak and slow to become angry . . ." (Jas 1:19). James would agree that we should seek to fully understand what others are saying before we seek to speak. Listening is mentioned first because it is one of the most important parts of communication, even more important than speaking.

James also wrote, "If anyone considers himself religious and yet does not keep a tight rein on his tongue, he deceives himself and his religion is worthless" (Jas 1:26). Keeping a tight rein on the tongue is not an easy proposition. It is like holding the reins while riding a horse. Not having a rein makes for a wild ride. In fact, the animal is in control. When it comes to the rein on the tongue, if we don't control it, our religion is worthless. These are some very strong words used here. I think James is serious in this passage when he uses the word "worthless."

Later in his letter James wrote, "We all stumble in many ways. If anyone is never at fault in what he says, he is a perfect man, able to keep his whole body in check" (Jas 3:2). People are at fault with what they say because they are responsible and accountable for every word they speak (see Matt 12:36). What should we say when we mess up in our communication? "I'm sorry" would be a great start. This is a very humbling statement for some people because they hate to admit they are wrong. Get a grip, swallow your pride, and heal the relationship by apologizing sincerely.

James continues about the tongue, "The tongue also is a fire, a world of evil among the parts of the body. It corrupts the whole person, sets the whole course of his life on fire, and is itself set on fire by hell" (Jas 3:6). The tongue can burn a person. This shows the tremendous power of the perverted tongue. The tongue can burn an individual's soul and spirit in a matter of a few seconds. The small "speech spark" can do a lot of damage to anyone within earshot, even to the speaker himself. Smokey Bear would say about the tongue, "Remember, only you can prevent family and friendship fires."

James continues his thoughts on communication by adding, "With the tongue we praise our Lord and Father, and with it we curse men, who have been made in God's likeness. Out of the same mouth come praise and cursing. My brothers, this should not be" (Jas 3:9-10). The mouth can curse and praise. It can destroy, devour, or heal a relationship. Ideally our tongue should only be used to glorify God and uplift others.

The last passage from James on communication is James 5:12, "Above all, my brothers, do not swear—not by heaven or by earth or by anything else. Let your 'Yes' be yes, and your 'No,' no, or you will be condemned." The passage echoes the condemnation his brother Jesus voiced about taking oaths or swearing that you are telling the truth. People get into trouble when they go beyond a simple "yes" or "no." They often feel that they owe people a fuller explanation. In some situations when we give people an explanation for an answer, we give them a way to attack and criticize us. Honesty should be our goal in conversing with others. Promises are to be kept: "yes" means yes. It is not a matter of discovering the meaning of "is." On the other hand, people can feel guilty about saying "no." This type of guilt is a false guilt. Keep speech simple!

Thoughts on Communication from Paul

Romans 3:13-14, "'Their throats are open graves; their tongues practice deceit.' 'The poison of vipers is on their lips.' 'Their mouths are full of cursing and bitterness.'" Just as graves contain vile and rotting corpses, so can our tongues produce rotten and putrid speech. Bitterness and cursing have become common expressions in communication today. All you have to do is listen to people to know that their unedifying speech is like a deadly poison that can destroy relationships.

Ephesians 4:15, "Instead, speaking the truth in love, we will in all things grow up into him who is the Head, that is, Christ." We can speak the truth without love, or love without the truth. Neither of these two communication patterns is appropriate.

Paul wrote in Ephesians 4:25-27 to put off falsehood and speak truthfully. At the same time he wrote about not sinning while you're angry and not letting the sun go down on your anger.

In Ephesians 4:29 Paul said not to let any unwholesome talk come out of the mouth. What types of conversation are unwholesome? Paul gives some examples in Ephesians 5:4,

"Nor should there be *obscenity, foolish talk* or *coarse joking,* which are out of place, but rather thanksgiving" (emphasis mine). Why is certain talk out of place and improper for God's people? Because it does not praise God, and it is not an appropriate witness. Paul says there should be no obscenity, foolish talk, or coarse joking. These are absolute standards, not situational ethics. A couple of months ago, I hurt my back. I was in so much pain that I couldn't get out of bed on my own. After debating with my wife about what should be done, the ambulance came to take me to the hospital (Janelle won the debate). The pain was beyond anything I had ever experienced. One of the EMTs told me it was okay to "cuss" when the pain was so bad. He was wrong! Cursing is wrong in any situation.

Colossians 3:8-9, "But now you must rid yourselves of all such things as these: anger, rage, malice, slander, and filthy language from your lips. Do not lie to each other, since you have taken off your old self with its practices." To improve communication we need to get rid of all of these things. You should never speak in anger. Speak only after you have cooled off. Resolve the conflict and your anger before the sun sets, or Satan will find a foothold (Eph 4:26-27). Lying is never an appropriate form of communication. Lying destroys relationships. Remember the old self was taken off when you became a Christian (2 Cor 5:17; Gal 2:20; Titus 3:1-7). Our old self includes our speech patterns. Our speech should be worthy of the One we represent.

Colossians 4:6, "Let your conversation be always full of grace, seasoned with salt, so that you may know how to answer everyone." Salt has many uses, three of which are purification, healing, and improving taste. Our words, like salt, can purify, heal, and improve communication conditions. They can also be full of grace, forgiveness, and mercy. The way we speak and what we speak about are a powerful witness for Christ.

Thoughts for the Week

Every word we speak should be kind and honoring. This should be the goal of all communication!

Anger ruins appropriate communication. Angry words are dangerous. Don't speak in anger. You must have and maintain peace before you communicate. Don't go to bed angry (Eph 4:16-17). Anger and bitterness ruin relationships and reputations (Matt 19:8).

Memory Verse for the Week

"Do not speak to a fool, for he will scorn the wisdom of your words" (Prov 23:9).

Chapter 13

The Power of the Word's Words

The Key to Christlike Communication: Christ

The Key to Christlike Communication: Christ

The Power of the Word's Words

Chapter 13

Who were the strangest communicators or possible communicators found in the Bible? Read about Balaam's talking donkey in Numbers 22:28-30. Jesus spoke about stones communicating when he entered Jerusalem on the day we call Palm Sunday (Luke 19:40).

As I close this book, I want to end it not with the strangest communicators but with the Great Communicator found in the Bible. The Bible contains literally thousands of communication statements made by Jesus. These statements are the gospel or the good news he brought to us. These statements deal with life, liberty, relationships, love, and eternal life. They convict, make you think, cause you to ponder, or offer hope.

The Gospel of John says it best, "In the beginning was the Word, and the Word was with God, and the Word was God. He was with God in the beginning. Through him all things were made; without him nothing was made that has been made. In him was life, and that life was the light of men. The light shines in the darkness, but the darkness has not understood it" (John 1:1-5). "The Word became flesh and made his dwelling among us. We have seen his glory, the glory of the One and Only, who came from the Father, full of grace and truth" (John 1:14). Jesus Christ is the literal expression of who God is in a form we can understand.

The writer of Hebrews taught this profound truth, "In the past God spoke to our forefathers through the prophets at many times and in various ways, but in these last days he has spoken to us by his Son, whom he appointed heir of all things, and through whom he made the universe. The Son is the radiance of God's glory and the exact representation of his being, sustaining all things by his powerful word. After he had provided purification for sins, he sat down at the right hand of the Majesty in heaven" (Heb 1:1-3).

What Jesus Said about His Teachings

John 3:11, "I tell you the truth, we speak of what we know, and we testify to what we have seen, but still you people do not accept our testimony."

John 3:31-36, "The one who comes from above is above all; the one who is from the earth belongs to the earth, and speaks as one from the earth. The one who comes from heaven is above all. He testifies to what he has seen and heard, but no one accepts his testimony. The man who has accepted it has certified that God is truthful. For the one whom God has sent speaks the words of God, for God gives the Spirit without limit. The Father loves the Son and has placed everything in his hands. Whoever believes in the Son has eternal life, but whoever rejects the Son will not see life, for God's wrath remains on him."

John 5:24, "I tell you the truth, whoever hears my word and believes him who sent me has eternal life and will not be condemned; he has crossed over from death to life."

John 5:37-40, "And the Father who sent me has himself testified concerning me. You have never heard his voice nor seen his form, nor does his word dwell in you, for you do not believe the one he sent. You diligently study the Scriptures because you think that by them you possess eternal life. These are the Scriptures that testify about me, yet you refuse to come to me to have life."

John 7:16-19, "Jesus answered, 'My teaching is not my own. It comes from him who sent me. If anyone chooses to do God's will, he will find out whether my teaching comes from God or whether I speak on my own. He who speaks on his own does so to gain honor for himself, but he who works for the honor of the one who sent him is a man of truth; there is nothing false about him. Has not Moses given you the law? Yet not one of you keeps the law. Why are you trying to kill me?'"

John 7:28, "Then Jesus, still teaching in the temple courts, cried out, 'Yes, you know me, and you know where I am from. I am not here on my own, but he who sent me is true. You do not know him.'"

John 8:14-18, "Jesus answered, 'Even if I testify on my own behalf, my testimony is valid, for I know where I came from and where I am going. But you have no idea where I come from or where I am going. You judge by human standards; I pass judgment on no one. But if I do judge, my decisions are right, because I am not alone. I stand with the Father, who sent me. In your own Law it is written that the testimony of two men is valid. I am one who testifies for myself; my other witness is the Father, who sent me.'"

John 8:28, "So Jesus said, 'When you have lifted up the Son of Man, then you will know that I am the one I claim to be and that I do nothing on my own but speak just what the Father has taught me.'"

John 12:49-50, "For I did not speak of my own accord, but the Father who sent me commanded me what to say and how to say it. I know that his command leads to eternal life. So whatever I say is just what the Father has told me to say."

John 14:10, "Don't you believe that I am in the Father, and that the Father is in me? The words I say to you are not just my own. Rather, it is the Father, living in me, who is doing his work."

John 14:24, "He who does not love me will not obey my teaching. These words you hear are not my own; they belong to the Father who sent me."

John 17:8, "For I gave them the words you gave me and they accepted them. They knew with certainty that I came from you, and they believed that you sent me."

John 17:14, "I have given them your word and the world has hated them, for they are not of the world any more than I am of the world."

In all these passages Jesus confirmed his authority to speak with God's voice. Jesus was the Master teacher, articulate with his spoken word. He taught with authority and not as one of the Pharisees and teachers of the law (Matt 7:28). At the same time he was gentle and compassionate (Matt 9:36; 11:28-30).

Jesus' Introductory Encounters

To Satan Jesus said, "It is written: 'Man does not live on bread alone, but on every word that comes from the mouth of God'" (Matt 4:4).

To Peter and Andrew, Jesus said, "Come, follow me, and I will make you fishers of men" (Matt 4:19).

When he began his preaching, it consisted of eight words: "Repent, for the kingdom of heaven is near" (Matt 4:17).

His first major sermon, referred to as "the Sermon on the Mount," is found in Matthew chapters 5–7. Depending on the translation, his message has only 2,443 English words in it. In this sermon Jesus addressed

Who Christians are (Matt 5:13-16)
How he came to fulfill the Law (5:17-20)
Murder, anger, and dispute resolution (5:21-26)
Adultery and divorce (5:27-32)
Keeping oaths and honest communication (5:33-37)
Justice and revenge (5:38-42)
Whom we should love (5:43-48)
Giving to help the poor (6:1-4)
Prayer (6:5-13)
Forgiveness (6:14-15)
Fasting (6:16-18)
Values and serving God (6:19-24)
Worry and priorities (6:25-34)
Judging others (7:1-5)
People not being ready to receive the gospel (7:6)
Prayer requests (7:7-11)
How to treat others (7:12)
How difficult the road to heaven is — that it is difficult to be a Christian and live the way you should (7:13-14)
Watching out for false teachings and teachers (7:15-23)
Building on a solid foundation and the consequences of a good or bad foundation (7:24-27)

This is quite comprehensive for a sermon, as written, that can be spoken in less than 20 minutes. When Jesus was finished with this sermon, Scripture says, "the crowds were amazed at his teaching, because he taught as one who had authority, and not as their teachers of the law" (7:28-29).

What made Jesus a great and authoritative communicator? A great communicator is not someone who tells you what you *want* to hear (2 Tim 4:3-4); it is someone who tells you what you don't want to hear, but persuades you that you need to. It is not someone who tickles ears, but someone who touches hearts. It is someone who cares enough to tell you the truth even though it might hurt your relationship (John 8:40; Gal 4:16).

Five Types of Questions/Statements

As a communicator, Jesus had a knack for helping people open up and reveal things to him. Jesus was an artist at asking open-ended questions that prompted people to share with him what was really going on.

? *informative*: These are for growing, learning, and developing (Matt 22:34-40).

? *accusatory*: "Have you stopped selling your body sexually to make money?" These questions are designed to trap/trip/trick (Matt 21:23; 22:15-17; John 8:3-6). Jesus answered this type of question with questions (Matt 21:24-25; 22:18-22).

? *insightful*: This is a question asked to get the person to hear his own answer (John 8:10).

? *confusing* and *causing doubt*: These are the ones that Satan likes. They usually begin with the words "did" or "if." He asks questions to create a great doubt debate inside the mind (Gen 3:1; Matt 4:3).

? *rhetorical*: This is a question asked merely for effect with no answer expected (Matt 6:27-28,30).

My Favorite Questions Jesus Asked

John 5:6 — "When Jesus saw him lying there and learned that he had been in this condition for a long time, he asked him,

'Do you want to get well?'" This is either the stupidest question in Scripture or the most insightful. Are there people in the world who like being sick? This is what I glean from Jesus' question. This man was paralyzed for 38 years. He should have wanted to get well, but maybe he preferred having other people do things for him and not having to be responsible for himself.

John 8:43 — "Why is my language not clear to you? Because you are unable to hear what I say."

Mark 3:4 — "Which is lawful on the Sabbath: to do good or to do evil, to save life or to kill?" The answer seems obvious!

Mark 6:38 — "'How many loaves do you have?' he asked. 'Go and see.' When they found out, they said, 'Five — and two fish.'" Jesus knew the answer; he wanted the disciples to know what they had to work with. He was going to use this to show them the power of God.

Luke 17:17-18 — "Were not all ten cleansed? Where are the other nine? Was no one found to return and give praise to God except this foreigner?"

Luke 18:41 — "What do you want me to do for you?"

Matthew 9:4-5 — "Why do you entertain evil thoughts in your hearts? Which is easier: to say, 'Your sins are forgiven,' or to say, 'Get up and walk'?"

Matthew 14:31 — "'You of little faith,' he said, 'why did you doubt?'"

Matthew 22:18 — "You hypocrites, why are you trying to trap me?"

John 21:15 — "Simon son of John, do you truly love me more than these?"

When Jesus met the woman at the well (John 4), why did he tell her to go get her husband? He was simply saying to her, "You can tell me the most painful events of your life and I will still care!" This had quite an impact on the woman (John 4:39). But it also had an impact on her town's people (John 4:40-42). I wonder what kind of words he spoke to them (v. 41). His words must have surprised them!

How could Jesus get her to open up so quickly? It was because he touched her in her hurting heart. Jesus made her feel safe and free to share her past with him. What a blessing! I wish we all could do this.

Look at how Jesus communicated with Mary in John 11:32-33, "When Mary reached the place where Jesus was and saw him, she fell at his feet and said, 'Lord, if you had been here, my brother would not have died.' When Jesus saw her weeping, and the Jews who had come along with her also weeping, he was deeply moved in spirit and troubled." Jesus did not stop her from saying what she believed to be true. How does this communication pattern relate to Romans 12:15-16? How did Jesus fulfill Galatians 6:2?

Jesus' Parables

Jesus also was an excellent communicator by using stories or parables. The word "parable" comes from the Greek *parabole*, which means placing beside or together as in a comparison.[1]

Parables
> House on rock or sand (Matt 7:24-27; Luke 6:47-49)
> The sowed seeds (Matt 13:3-9; Mark 4:3-8; Luke 8:5-15)
> The tares (Matt 13:24-30)
> The mustard seed (Matt 13:31-32; Mark 4:30-32; Luke 13:18-19)
> The yeast (Matt 13:33; Luke 13:20-21)
> The hidden treasure (Matt 13:44)
> The pearl of great price (Matt 13:45)

The net (Matt 13:47-50)

The lost sheep (Matt 18:12-14; Luke 15:4-7)

The unmerciful servant (Matt 18:23-35)

The workers in the vineyard (Matt 20:1-16)

The two sons (Matt 21:28-32)

The wicked tenants (Matt 21:33-40; Mark 12:1-11; Luke 20:9-16)

The marriage of the prince (Matt 22:2-14)

The fig tree (Matt 24:32-34; Mark 13:28-29; Luke 21:29-31)

The ten virgins (Matt 25:1-13)

The talents (Matt 25:14-30)

The sheep and goats (Matt 25:31-46)

The seed (Mark 4:26-29)

The householder (Mark 13:34)

The two debtors (Luke 7:41)

The good Samaritan (Luke 10:30-37)

The persistent friend request (Luke 11:5-8)

The rich fool (Luke 12:16-21)

The watching servants (Luke 12:35-40)

The wise steward (Luke 12:42-48)

The fig tree (Luke 13:6-9)

The great banquet (Luke 14:16-24)

The tower, going off to war (Luke 14:28-32)

The lost coin (Luke 15:8-10)

The prodigal son (Luke 15:11-32)

The shrewd manager (Luke 16:1-13)

The rich man and Lazarus (Luke 16:19-31)

The unprofitable servants (Luke 17:7-10)

The unjust judge and persistent widow (Luke 18:2-8)

The Pharisee and sinner (Luke 18:10-14)

The ten minas (Luke 19:12-27)

Analogies

The candle under a bushel (Matt 5:15; Mark 4:21; Luke 8:16; 11:33)

The new cloth on old garment (Matt 9:16; Mark 2:21; Luke 5:36)

New wine and old wineskin (Matt 9:17; Mark 2:22; Luke 5:37)

Things I Wish Jesus Had Not Said

Jesus made many statements that make you search your soul. Many statements convict. Many statements shake the spiritual foundation. He just could not leave well enough alone. That is why I wish he had not said these things.

In Matthew 5:21-22,27-28,31-32,33-34,38-42,43-44 Jesus changes the Ten Commandments and makes them even more difficult to attain by human efforts. In all of these verses Jesus said, "But I tell you." He was teaching that we cannot attain what God wants without him. I personally have not broken most of the original Ten Commandments, but with Jesus' updated ones I don't fare as well. I have never coveted my neighbor's donkey. I am blessed because he does not have one.

Many of the statements and teachings mentioned below are very colorful and meaningful. These promises and statements add a lot to a person's life if one takes them to heart.

Matthew 6:15 — "But if you do not forgive men their sins, your Father will not forgive your sins."

Matthew 7:1-2 — "Do not judge, or you too will be judged. For in the same way you judge others, you will be judged, and with the measure you use, it will be measured to you."

Matthew 12:36-37 — "But I tell you that men will have to give account on the day of judgment for every careless word they have spoken. For by your words you will be acquitted, and by your words you will be condemned."

Mark 8:34-38 — "If anyone would come after me, he must deny himself and take up his cross and follow me. For whoever wants to save his life will lose it, but whoever loses his life for me and for the gospel will save it. What good is it for a man to gain the whole world, yet forfeit his soul? Or what can a man give in exchange for his soul? If anyone is ashamed of me and my words in this adulterous and sinful generation, the Son of Man will be ashamed of him when he comes in his Father's glory with the holy angels."

Luke 14:26-27 — "If anyone comes to me and does not hate his father and mother, his wife and children, his brothers and sisters — yes, even his own life — he cannot be my disciple. And anyone who does not carry his cross and follow me cannot be my disciple."

John 14:6 — "I am the way and the truth and the life. No one comes to the Father except through me." If Jesus had not said this, this would mean that people would have a chance to find God and heaven through other ways.

Things I Am Glad Jesus Said

Jesus said many beautiful things that improve our outlook and relationship with God. That is why I am glad Jesus made these statements. His compassion and love are obvious in them. God is simply awesome!

Matthew 5:11-12 — "Blessed are you when people insult you, persecute you and falsely say all kinds of evil against you because of me. Rejoice and be glad, because great is your reward in heaven, for in the same way they persecuted the prophets who were before you."

Matthew 6:9-13 — "This, then, is how you should pray: 'Our Father in heaven, hallowed be your name, your kingdom come, your will be done on earth as it is in heaven. Give us today our daily bread. Forgive us our debts, as we also have forgiven our debtors. And lead us not into temptation, but deliver us from the evil one.'"

Matthew 6:33-34 — "But seek first his kingdom and his righteousness, and all these things will be given to you as well. Therefore do not worry about tomorrow, for tomorrow will worry about itself. Each day has enough trouble of its own."

Matthew 7:12 — "So in everything, do to others what you would have them do to you, for this sums up the Law and the Prophets."

Matthew 13:44-46 — "The kingdom of heaven is like treasure hidden in a field. When a man found it, he hid it again, and then in his joy went and sold all he had and bought that field. Again, the kingdom of heaven is like a merchant looking for fine pearls. When he found one of great value, he went away and sold everything he had and bought it."

Matthew 21:21-22 — "Jesus replied, 'I tell you the truth, if you have faith and do not doubt, not only can you do what was done to the fig tree, but also you can say to this mountain, "Go, throw yourself into the sea," and it will be done. If you believe, you will receive whatever you ask for in prayer.'"

Matthew 22:21 — "Give to Caesar what is Caesar's, and give to God what is God's."

Matthew 22:37-40 — "'Love the Lord your God with all your heart and with all your soul and with all your mind.' This is the first and greatest commandment. And the second is like it: 'Love your neighbor as yourself.' All the Law and the Prophets hang on these two commandments."

Matthew 23:24 — "You blind guides! You strain out a gnat but swallow a camel."

Matthew 25:21 — "His master replied, 'Well done, good and faithful servant! You have been faithful with a few things; I will put you in charge of many things. Come and share your master's happiness!'"

Matthew 28:20 — ". . . And surely I am with you always, to the very end of the age."

Mark 5:19 — "Jesus did not let him, but said, 'Go home to your family and tell them how much the Lord has done for you, and how he has had mercy on you.'"

Mark 6:50 — "Take courage! It is I. Don't be afraid."

Luke 5:20-24 — "When Jesus saw their faith, he said, 'Friend, your sins are forgiven.' The Pharisees and the teachers of the law began thinking to themselves, 'Who is this fellow who speaks blasphemy? Who can forgive sins but God alone?' Jesus knew what they were thinking and asked, 'Why are you thinking these things in your hearts? Which is easier: to say, 'Your sins are forgiven,' or to say, 'Get up and walk'? But that you may know that the Son of Man has authority on earth to forgive sins. . . .' He said to the paralyzed man, 'I tell you, get up, take your mat and go home.'"

Luke 6:31 — "Do to others as you would have them do to you."

Luke 7:28 — "I tell you, among those born of women there is no one greater than John; yet the one who is least in the kingdom of God is greater than he."

John 3:16 — "For God so loved the world that he gave his one and only Son, that whoever believes in him shall not perish but have eternal life."

John 4:13-14 — "Jesus answered, 'Everyone who drinks this water will be thirsty again, but whoever drinks the water I give him will never thirst. Indeed, the water I give him will become in him a spring of water welling up to eternal life.'"

John 8:32 — "Then you will know the truth, and the truth will set you free."

John 11:25 — "Jesus said to her, 'I am the resurrection and the life. He who believes in me will live, even though he dies.'"

John 13:34-35 — "A new command I give you: Love one another. As I have loved you, so you must love one another. By this all men will know that you are my disciples, if you love one another."

John 15:11 — "I have told you this so that my joy may be in you and that your joy maybe complete."

John 16:33 — "I have told you these things, so that in me you may have peace. In this world you will have trouble. But take heart! I have overcome the world."

I know that I gave you a lot of verses in the above section. I am awed by what the Word of God says. I tremble in excitement about what it teaches.

Eleven words can change a life. Jesus said, "Zacchaeus, come down immediately. I must stay at your house today" (Luke 19:5). These words, and the actions that went with them, had a tremendous impact on Zacchaeus. He said to Jesus, "Look, Lord! Here and now I give half of my possessions to the poor, and if I have cheated anybody out of anything, I will pay back four times the amount" (Luke 19:8). Jesus then told him that "salvation has come to this house" (Luke 19:9).

Famous Last Words

In my senior year of high school there was the "last will and testament." given right before graduation. Seniors could will things to the junior class. At times these "wills" were funny, serious, or crude. These were going to be the last words the seniors spoke to the juniors, sophomores and freshmen.

Last words mean a lot. Can you think of the last words spoken by people in the Bible? Here are some of them:

Jacob's last words were blessings to his children (Gen 48:15–49:28).

Moses' last words were a blessing to the tribes of Israel (Deut 33:1-29).

Acts 1:8 — "But you will receive power when the Holy Spirit comes on you; and you will be my witnesses in Jerusalem, and in all Judea and Samaria, and to the ends of the earth." Jesus spoke about power and witnessing.

James 5:20 — "Remember this: Whoever turns a sinner from the error of his way will save him from death and cover over a multitude of sins." James spoke on witnessing.

2 Peter 3:18 — "But grow in the grace and knowledge of our Lord and Savior Jesus Christ. To him be glory both now and forever! Amen." Peter spoke on growth, grace, and Christ's glory.

Jude 24-25 — "To him who is able to keep you from falling and to present you before his glorious presence without fault and with great joy — to the only God our Savior be glory, majesty, power and authority, through Jesus Christ our Lord, before all ages, now and forevermore! Amen." Jude thought about Jesus' presenting Christians before God at the end times.

John, known for emphasizing grace, Revelation 22:21 — "The grace of the Lord Jesus be with God's people. Amen."

Thought for the Week

Be sure to think about what you are going to say, or you can be sure you will say something before you think. Guard your heart (Prov 4:23).

Memory Verses for the Week

"True instruction was in his mouth and nothing false was found on his lips. He walked with me in peace and uprightness, and turned many from sin. For the lips of a priest ought to preserve knowledge, and from his mouth men should seek instruction—because he is the messenger of the LORD Almighty" (Malachi 2:6-7).

"When the Lord brought back the captives to Zion, we were like men who dreamed. Our mouths were filled with laughter, our tongues with songs of joy. Then it was said among the nations, 'The Lord has done great things for them.' The Lord has done great things for us, and we are filled with joy" (Ps 126:1-3).

Endnote

1. F.N. Peloubet, *Peloubet's Bible Dictionary* (Philadelphia: Universal Book and Bible House, 1925), p. 484.

Selected Bibliography

Alderson, Wayne T., and Nancy Alderson. *Theory R Management*. Nashville, TN: Thomas Nelson, 1994.

Carter, Jimmy. *Living Faith*. New York: Times Books, a division of Random House, Inc., n.d.

Durham, Ken. *Speaking from the Heart: Richer Relationships through Communication*. Ft. Worth: Sweet, 1986.

Godek, Gregory J.P. *1001 Ways to Be Romantic*. Boston: Casablanca Press, 1995.

Hammond, Corydon D., Dean H. Hepworth, and Veon G. Smith. *Improving Therapeutic Communication*. San Francisco: Jossey-Bass Publishers, 1978.

Hekker, Terry. *Ever Since Adam and Eve*. New York: William Morrow and Co., 1979.

Henry, Carl F.H., ed. *Baker's Dictionary of Christian Ethics*. Grand Rapids: Baker, 1973.

Jaffray, Norman R. "Good Listener," *Saturday Evening Post*, December 6, 1958.

LaHaye, Tim. *How to Be Happy through Marriage*. Wheaton, IL: Tyndale, 1971.

Lucado, Max. *Life Lessons with Max Lucado — Book of James*. Dallas: Word, 1996.

McLellan, Vern. *Quips, Quotes and Quests*. Eugene, OR: Harvest House, 1982.

Mischel, Walter. *Introductions to Personality*. 2nd ed. New York: Holt, Rinehart and Winston, 1979.

Osborne, Cecil G. *The Art of Understanding Your Mate*. Grand Rapids: Zondervan, 1970.

Packer, James I., Merrill C. Tenney, and William White, eds. *The Bible Almanac*. Carmel, NY: Guideposts (by special arrangement with Thomas Nelson), 1980.

Parrott, Les, III. *High-Maintenance Relationships: How to Handle Impossible People.* Wheaton, IL: Tyndale, 1996.

Peloubet, F.N. *Peloubet's Bible Dictionary.* Philadelphia: Universal Book and Bible House, 1925.

Powell, John. *Why Am I Afraid to Tell You Who I Am?* Allen, TX: Argus Communications, 1969.

Smalley, Gary. *Hidden Keys of a Loving Lasting Marriage.* Grand Rapids: Zondervan, 1984.

Smalley, Gary, and Dr. John Trent. *The Two Sides of Love.* Pomona, CA: Focus on the Family Publishing, 1990.

Swindoll, Charles R. *The Mystery of God's Will: What Does He Want for Me?* Nashville: Word, 1999.

_____. *Strike the Original Match: Rekindling and Preserving Your Marriage Fire.* Portland, OR: Multnomah Press, 1980.

Tan, Paul Lee. *Encyclopedia of 7,700 Illustrations: Signs of the Times.* Rockville, MD: Assurance Publishers, 1984.

Thatcher, Floyd and Harriett. *Long-term Marriage: A Search for the Ingredients of a Lifetime Partnership.* Waco, TX: Word, 1983.

Vine, W.E., Merrill F. Unger, and William White, Jr. *Vine's Complete Expository Dictionary of Old and New Testament Words.* Nashville: Thomas Nelson, 1985.

Whitney, Donald S. *Spiritual Disciplines for the Christian Life.* Colorado Springs: Navpress, 1991.

Wright, H. Norman. *Communication: Key to Your Marriage.* Ventura, CA: Regal Books, 1980.

Wurman, Richard Saul. *Information Anxiety.* New York: Doubleday, 1998.

Zodhiates, Spiros. *The Complete Word Study Dictionary — New Testament.* Chattanooga, TN: AMG, 1992.

_____, ed. *The Hebrew–Greek Key Study Bible.* Chattanooga, TN: AMG, 1990.

Appendix

Outtakes

We have all seen the clips of outtakes from movies and television programs—shots that were taken which for whatever reason were not used in the final film. In the course of putting a book together materials are moved, edited, cut, and deleted. Not everything one starts with ends up as part of the finished product. Most of what is shown on television and sometimes at the ends of movies as outtakes are usually funny things where the actors messed up and had to try again. This Appendix represents a few outtakes from the original manuscript of this book.

Apropos Anagrams

Anagrams illustrate how words and thoughts can be changed, manipulated, and misinterpreted. Anagrams are words formed by rearranging letters from other words or phrases. Some can come close to being synonymous with the source word or words:

dirty room	dormitory
slot machines	cash lost in em
mother-in-law	woman Hitler
snooze alarms	alas no more Zs
semolina	is no meal
the public art galleries	large picture halls, I bet
astronomer	moon starer
eleven plus two	twelve plus one
contradiction	accord not in it
year two thousand	a year to shut down

Words with Wallop

Wilfred Funk, a noted lexicographer and dictionary publisher, suggests the ten most *impressive* words in the English language.

"Alone" — the bitterest word
"Mother" — the most revered word
"Death" — the most tragic
"Faith" — brings greatest comfort
"Forgotten" — saddest
"Love" — most beautiful
"Revenge" — cruelest
"Friendship" — warmest
"No" — coldest
"Tranquillity" — most peaceful[1]

Quirky Quixotic Quiz

1. How long was the Hundred Years War?
2. Which country makes Panama hats?
3. From what animal do we get catgut?

4. In what month do Russians celebrate the October Revolution?
5. From what material are camel's hair brushes made?
6. The Canary Islands in the Pacific are named after what animal?
7. What was King George VI's first name?
8. What color is a purple finch?
9. Where do we get Chinese gooseberries from?
10. How long did the Thirty Years War last?

Answers
1. 116 years, from 1337 to 1453
2. Ecuador
3. Sheep and horses
4. November. The Russian calendar was 13 days behind ours.
5. Squirrel fur.
6. The Latin name was Insularia Canaria—Island of the Dogs. The birds were named for the islands.
7. Albert. In 1936 he respected the wish of Queen Victoria that no future king should ever be called Albert.
8. Crimson.
9. New Zealand and California. Chinese gooseberries were renamed kiwis by marketers in New Zealand where they are grown commercially (also in California), but they do originate from China and Taiwan.
10. Thirty years, of course, from 1618 to 1648.

Legal Language

A new law has taken effect in the 66 school parishes in Louisiana. This law mandates respectful conversations with teachers, school employees, and students. Students have to address these people with "ma'am" or "sir." Individual school parishes will determine the punishment for students who don't follow this law. The only restriction made in the law is that the students can't be expelled or suspended.[2]

Endnotes

1. Tan, *Encyclopedia of 7,700 Illustrations,* pp. 1411-1412.
2. Associated Press (August 21, 1999).

About the Author

Charles Gerber, MA, is the founder and executive director of Christian Counseling Services in Muncie, Indiana. He has authored three other books for College Press and is a popular national speaker.

Charley speaks nationally on the topic of communication as well as other topics related to Christian counseling. He has presented seminars and workshops at churches and conventions on a variety of mental health-related subjects.

Charley lives in Muncie with his wife, Janelle, and his two children, Joshua and Caitlyn. He is an elder at University Christian Church in Muncie, IN.

Contact Information

Christian Counseling Services
1804 North Wheeling Ave.
Muncie, Indiana 47303

(765) 289-1631

email: CCSCharley@aol.com

Christ-Centered Self-Esteemed
Seeing Ourselves through God's Eyes
Charles R. Gerber

This work is an excellent resource to help you see yourself as God sees you. Several examples are cited from the Scriptures, examining both positive and negative esteem characteristics. This book will change the way you look at yourself, and thus, change the way you relate to others. Read it today!

179 pages, soft, #G01-649-3, $9.99

Healing for a Bitter Heart
Releasing the Power of Forgiveness
Charles R. Gerber

Harboring bitterness will slowly destroy a person's life, and wreak havoc on relationships. God has demonstrated the power of forgiveness. You can learn the power of that forgiveness in your own life. If you struggle with the issue of forgiveness, or if you know someone who does, this book is a must read. Stop living in the life-draining grip of bitterness. God wants you to live a better life. This book will help you understand that truth and take steps to change your life for the better.

312 pages, soft, #G01-787-2, $12.99

CHARLES R. GERBER

LIVING WITH
STRESS

Biblical Truths to Manage Your Life

Living with Stress
Biblical Truths to Manage Your Life
Charles R. Gerber

Have you ever felt stressed out? Everyone does at one point or another, it just comes with being alive. Some stress gets you ready for the day's experiences (I want to get to work on time). Other stress can have negative influences on your life (the speeding ticket received while trying to get to work on time). Our perspective toward how we view various stress points will determine whether stress is helpful or hurtful. If we learn the biblical principles of dealing with stress, we will be equipped to live holy and happy lives.

120 pages, soft, $9.99